D1406697

Chancellorsville to Appomattox

The Battles of 1863 to 1865

Chancellorsville to Appomattox

The Battles of 1863 to 1865

The House Divided
The Civil War

Corinne J. Naden & Rose Blue

RSVP

RAINTREE
STECK-VAUGHN
PUBLISHERS
A Steck-Vaughn Company

Austin, Texas

www.steck-vaughn.com

For Maire Plunkett Baldwin, my favorite college kid, with love, from Corinne
For my very good friend Sam Roth, with love, from Rose

Published by Raintree Steck-Vaughn Publishers,
an imprint of Steck-Vaughn Company

Publishing Director: Walter Kossmann
Editor: Shirley Shalit
Project Management & Design: Gino Coverty
Cover Design: Gino Coverty
Media Researcher: Claudette Landry
Electronic Production: Scott Melcer
Consultant: Paul Finkelman, University of Tulsa, College of Law

Library of Congress Cataloging-in-Publication Data

Naden, Corinne. J.
    Chancellorsville to Appomattox: battles of 1863 to 1865 / Corinne
J. Naden & Rose Blue.
      p.   cm. — (The house divided)
    Includes bibliographical references (p.   ) and index.
    Summary: Describes battles and events in the latter years of the
Civil War, from the Battle of Chancellorsville to Sherman's march on
Atlanta and the end of the war.
    ISBN 0-8172-5582-6
    1. United States — History — Civil War, 1861–1865 — Campaigns
Juvenile literature.   [1. United States — History — Civil War, 1861–1865 —
Campaigns.]   I. Blue, Rose.   II. Title.   III. Series: Naden, Corinne J.
House divided.
E470.N35   2000
973.7'3 — DC21   99-15597
                                                         CIP
Printed and bound in the United States of America
1 2 3 4 5 6 7 8 9 0 IP 03 02 01 00 99

Cover photo: The Battle of Gettysburg, July 3, 1863
Title page photo: Lee's surrender at Appomattox Court House, Virginia

Acknowledgments listed on page 112 constitute part of this copyright page.

Contents

The Strange Document

Prologue

As of January 1, 1863,

> ...all persons held as slaves within any State, or designated part of a State, the people whereof shall then be in rebellion against the United States, shall be then, thenceforward, and forever free.

That was the gist of the Emancipation Proclamation, issued by Abraham Lincoln on September 22, 1862, five days after the battle of Antietam. It was a statement of intent. If the states that left the Union did not return to it as of January 1, 1863, their slaves would be declared free. Lincoln felt that if his name went into history, it would be for this act alone. As it turned out, history remembers him for many deeds, although the Emancipation Proclamation is indeed one of America's most important documents. Yet, for all that, it is also one of the strangest.

For one thing, it freed the slaves who were in the Confederacy—"those States in rebellion." But Lincoln had no way to back up that declaration, except, of course, by winning the war, which he certainly had not done by January 1, 1863. Also, it did not apply to the border states that were on the side of the Union. Slaves in Delaware, Maryland, Kentucky, and Missouri would remain slaves. It would not apply to the area of northwestern Virginia, which was to join the Union as a separate state on June 20, 1863. Nor would parts of Louisiana and much

The first reading of the Emancipation Proclamation before Lincoln's Cabinet on September 22, 1862

of Tennessee be affected as they were back under control of the U.S. government. In addition, was it legal? Basically, the national government had no power over slavery in the states. Yet, strictly as a war measure, restricted to areas "in rebellion," as commander in chief, Lincoln could—and did—declare free the slaves owned by masters in rebellion. But legal or not, the Emancipation Proclamation proved to be a very powerful document indeed. Prodded by his lifelong hostility to slavery and the strong antislavery views of most of his party's leaders, Lincoln felt the time was right. He also believed that the war did not have the total, vigorous support of the people. They needed a stronger rallying cry than "preserving the Union." The federal government must take an official stand against slavery. The Emancipation Proclamation did just that. However, Lincoln was advised not to issue it until the North had won a decisive victory; otherwise it might sound merely like a cry for help. Northern victories were hard to come by in late 1862, but after the bloody battle at Antietam in September, Lincoln issued his Proclamation.

FIRST WINNER

Sergeant William H. Carney, 23 years old , was the first black to win the Congressional Medal of Honor in the Civil War. He was part of the 54th Massachusetts—the Glory Brigade, a black regiment led by 25 year old Robert G. Shaw, a white colonel. Shaw was anxious to prove the ability of his men to fight, which many in the military doubted. The Glory Brigade led the charge on Fort Wagner, South Carolina, in July 1863. Carney, wounded twice, recovered, but Shaw died in the assault. The Confederates buried him with his black soldiers to shame him. Instead, it made him a greater hero in the North. Said Shaw's father, "We can imagine no holier place than that in which he is, among his brave and devoted followers, nor wish for him better company." The Glory Brigade demonstrated the ability of black soldiers and Shaw demonstrated the commitment of many Northerners to ending slavery. Other white officers also volunteered to lead black troops for the North.

Sergeant William Carney holding the flag of his brigade.

It had two immediate effects, one practical, one more psychological. On the practical side, it was a go-ahead signal to recruit blacks into the Federal army. By the end of the war, some 186,000 black soldiers had put on the Union blue. At least 20,000 served in the U.S. Navy, and thousands more were in noncombatant roles. More than 32,000 died and more than 20 earned the Congressional Medal of Honor for their bravery.

On the more psychological and even more powerful side, the Emancipation Proclamation helped to swing foreign opinion toward the North and away from the South. How could Great Britain or France go on record as opposing a nation that opposed slavery? After the Proclamation, the chance that Britain would support the Confederacy grew slimmer and slimmer and finally vanished altogether. It was not that Great Britain or France actually favored the North. Britain had a nasty habit, as the Union saw it, of building ships for the Confederacy, such as the *Alabama* and *Shenandoah*. The British also needed Southern cotton, although by 1863 they were getting most of their cotton from India and Egypt. What Britain needed more, after several years of bad growing seasons in Europe, was Northern wheat. That, coupled with reluctance to come out against a declaration of antislavery, tended to keep Great Britain from taking part in the conflict.

France, led by Emperor Napoleon III, was a bit more of a problem. He was openly quite friendly to the Confederacy and, in 1862, suggested that Britain, Russia, and France try to arrange a cease-fire. He also suggested that if the North objected, perhaps it was time for foreign intervention. Britain and Russia were having none of that and neither was the U.S. Congress, which firmly told the French emperor that his suggestion was an "unfriendly act." Napoleon probably would have welcomed a Southern victory because his real interest was Mexico where, in 1864, he would install the Austrian archduke Maximilian as emperor, propped up by French troops. This was in direct violation of the Monroe Doctrine, which forbid foreign powers from interfering in the internal affairs of Western Hemisphere nations. When the U.S. government, shortly after the end of the Civil War, sent American troops to the Mexican border as a warning, Napoleon withdrew his troops. This toppled

THE ARMY'S NOT FOR ME

Wrote Private Delos W. Lake, 19th Michigan, in a letter home: "The army is the worst place in the world to learn bad habbits of all kinds. There is several men in this Regt. when they enlisted they were nice respectable men and belonged to the Church of God, but now where are they? There are ruined men."

Maximilian, who was executed, and the Mexicans took back their country.

The most pro-North of the three European nations turned out to be czarist Russia. The Union was pleased when Russia sent one fleet to New York Harbor and another to San Francisco to spend the winter of 1863. It did, indeed, seem like a warning to the South. Actually, Russia was not on the best of terms at the time with Great Britain or France and didn't want to risk having its ships stuck in the ice of its own ports.

And so, the third year of the American Civil War opened with a declaration that freed the slaves. It was perhaps the single most important document of the war, and the fallout from it doomed the South. But, for now, as the new year began, only more fighting, more bloodshed, and more deaths lay ahead. The Army of the Potomac was miserably encamped at Falmouth, Virginia, under command of General Ambrose E. Burnside. Still vivid in his mind was the defeat suffered in December at Fredericksburg. As for the soldiers, they were so homesick that about 200 a day deserted; and the camps were so unhealthy that two men died from disease for every one killed in battle. Poor food, long marches in ill-fitting shoes, and the boredom of inactivity contributed to their low morale.

The South wasn't having an easy time either, not with its government and not with its army. About the only thing that the Confederate Congress seemed to agree on was that nobody liked President Jefferson Davis. As for Davis, he had an astonishing facility for making enemies. He constantly quarreled with his

military leaders and spent endless hours agonizing over every decision. Perhaps the Atlanta *Southern Confederacy* had Davis in mind when it wrote, "If we are defeated, it will be by the people at home." In Davis's defense, he certainly did not have an easy job. He was the head of a declared nation made up of 11 states that had not the slightest inclination toward central government. Davis proclaimed a national day of fasting for the war effort. One governor refused and named his own fast day. The governor of South Carolina argued when officers from one of the other states sometimes commanded his own troops in battle. Food was scarce and prices out of sight. By mid-1863, a bar of soap cost $1.10, or one-tenth of a soldier's monthly pay. By year's end, a barrel of flour cost $250. Schools shut down because so many students and teachers were off fighting, or because there was no money to pay teachers.

The boys in gray had some of the same problems as their Northern counterparts. Desertion was rampant. By the end of 1863, about two-fifths of the Confederate army was absent, with or without leave. But the fighting and the dying continued. So did the bravery and the bloodshed. Victory was still hoped for by both sides, and the Civil War still had nearly a year and a half to go.

Chancellorsville:

Death of a Hero
May 1–4, 1863

The new year opened with the Battle of Murfreesboro, or Stone's River, Tennessee, on January 2. The Confederate Army of Tennessee was commanded by General Braxton Bragg, a veteran of the Battle of Shiloh the preceding April. Opposing him was Major General William S. Rosecrans, Army of the Mississippi. The cost of this two-day battle was horrendous. The North lost nearly 13,000 men—killed, wounded, or missing; the South, more than 11,500. After notifying Richmond that he had won, the unpredictable Bragg failed to renew the attack and left the battlefield. The Federal troops remained and called it a victory. However, Rosecrans's army was so badly mangled that it would be effectively out of action for six months. Few battles of the Civil War cost more or meant less.

NO END IN SIGHT

Wrote a Confederate soldier after Murfreesboro: "I am sick and tired of this war, and, I can see no prospects of having peace for a long time to come, I don't think it ever will be stopped by fighting, the Yankees cant whip us and we can never whip them, and I see no prospect of peace unless the Yankees themselves rebell and throw down their arms, and refuse to fight any longer."

Later that month, President Lincoln named a new commander for the Army of the Potomac. Major General Joseph Hooker replaced Ambrose Burnside. This was not unexpected. General Burnside, who didn't want the job in the first place, had been defeated by Robert E. Lee at Fredericksburg and for the past month had been mired down in the mud of a Virginia winter. His army was depressed and dispirited. Unlike Burnside, however, Hooker really wanted the job.

He had fought at Second Bull Run, at Antietam, and Fredericksburg. The general from Massachusetts was known as a courageous fighter. He was also known, unfortunately, as a big drinker with a big mouth.

Hooker immediately set about the task of rebuilding the Army of the Potomac. He cleaned up the camps, got the men paid, tightened discipline, and devised a plan to defeat the elusive General Lee. All in all, Hooker was quite pleased with himself, announcing that "My plans are perfect. May God have mercy on General Lee, for I will have none."

Hooker intended to leave Falmouth as soon as weather permitted and send one part of his army to attack Lee, still at Fredericksburg, from the front. Most of the Federal forces, however, would march along the Rappahannock River, cross it to attack Lee from the rear, destroy his army, and head for the Confederate capital of Richmond, Virginia.

"I WANT YOU— I THINK"

President Lincoln was not unaware of Hooker's virtues—and faults. He wrote to the general before he assumed command on January 26, 1863: "There are some things in regard to which, I am not quite satisfied with you. I believe you to be a brave and skilful soldier, which, of course I like.... I have heard, in such way as to believe it, of your recently saying that both the Army and the Government needed a Dictator. Of course, it was not for this, but in spite of it, that I have given you the command. Only those generals who gain successes, can set up dictators. What I now ask of you is military success, and I will risk the dictatorship."

Hooker's enthusiasm rippled throughout his officer corps. The men began to talk as though Lee were already defeated. Lincoln, although pleased with his general's initiative, was a bit more cautious. The President remarked, "The hen is the wisest of all animal creation, because she never cackles until after the egg is laid."

While the Army of the Potomac got ready for its big push, small battles were being fought throughout the South, in Mississippi, Tennessee, Arkansas, and Florida. Late in January, the Confederate ship *Alabama* seized a Federal vessel off the coast of Central America. On January 30, a Federal gunboat was captured near Charleston, and the following day two Confederate gunboats left Charleston harbor and severely damaged two Northern ships.

Much of the history of the Civil War focuses on the land battles since that is where so much of the fighting occurred. But those on the sea played an important role as well. Seapower by itself did not decide the outcome of the Civil War, but, coupled with the land forces, it gave a great advantage to the North. When the war began, the world's navies were adjusting to the change from sail to steam, and by the war's end they were changing from wooden to iron ships. At the start of the war, the South had no navy at all, the North about 90 warships. Some 40 were steam-driven, some were badly in need of repair, some

General Joseph Hooker poses stiffly on horseback to have his photograph taken.

14

were in foreign ports, some were out of commission, including its five powerful steam frigates.

With this force, the North intended to blockade more than 3,500 miles of Confederate coastline and control traffic on the Mississippi and Tennessee Rivers. When the fighting started, Lincoln immediately announced a blockade of all Southern ports, even though such an order would be difficult to carry out. However, by using anything that could float and spending a good deal of money, the blockade eventually became highly effective, although never airtight, by the end of the war. Given time, the blockade would slowly strangle the South.

Beginning with the most famous naval engagement of the war —the battle of the ironclads, the North's *Monitor* and the South's *Merrimac*, rechristened *Virginia*—on March 9, 1861, the Confederacy acquitted itself admirably. That battle ended in a draw. The surprise is not that the South did so poorly with what navy it had, but that it did so well. Short of almost everything, including shipbuilding facilities, trained mechanics, and materials, the South still managed to inflict a good deal of damage, although never enough to change the outcome of the war.

The grand prize of the Union blockade was the port city of New Orleans, Louisiana. To capture it would mean cutting off the major Southern outlet to foreign markets. New Orleans fell on April 25, 1862, when 43 ships under the command of Admiral David G. Farragut entered the lower Mississippi River. Resistance was useless and 15,000 Federal troops took over the city on May 1. Their leader, General B.F. Butler, was later criticized by pro-Confederate whites for his harsh military rule.

Farragut became a naval hero. Tough, intelligent, and still fit at age 61, he had been viewed with some suspicion at the beginning of the war and was assigned to a desk job in Washington. That was because this Tennessee native had family ties both in

men burst from the Wilderness, causing the disorderly retreat of the Northern troops. The Battle of Chancellorsville would continue for two more days. In the end, the South took an unexpected victory and Hooker's perfect plan ended in defeat. Once more, one of Lincoln's generals had failed him.

Hooker lost 17,000 men, killed, wounded, or missing, at the Battle of Chancellorsville. An army half the size of his had cut him to pieces. The Army of the Potomac drew back across the Rappahannock River. The elusive drive on Richmond seemed farther away than ever.

Chancellorsville was one of Lee's most brilliant victories of the war. The cost, however, was tremendous. Nearly 13,000 Confederates were killed, wounded, or listed as missing. And as terrible as those losses were, General Lee had to endure another, even more personal tragedy.

In the shadowy darkness of the Wilderness on the night of May 2, Stonewall Jackson and two of his officers were mistaken for the enemy and shot by their own men. The officers died, and Jackson was hit three times, twice in his left arm and once in his right hand. The arm could not be saved, and the next morning it was amputated. Said a horrified Lee, "Jackson has lost his left arm, but I have lost my right."

Jackson was taken to a farmhouse near Guiney Station, Virginia, to recuperate. But suddenly he developed pneumonia, and his wife was sent for. On the afternoon of Sunday, May 10, after dozing on and off, he opened his eyes and said, "Let us cross over the river and rest under the shade of the trees." Then he died.

Lee lost his closest military comrade and knew not how to replace him. The South lost one of its greatest generals. Jackson was buried, as he had asked, at the Virginia Military Institute, where he had taught before the war, "in Lexington, in the Valley of Virginia." Flags dipped in mourning throughout the

STONEWALL JACKSON'S LAST BATTLE

Captain and Reverend James Power Smith wrote of Jackson's death, "As he [Jackson] rode near to the Confederate troops, just placed in position and ignorant that he was in the front, the left company began firing to the front, and two of his party fell from their saddles dead ... he was met by a second volley ... The large bone of the upper arm was splintered to the elbow-joint, and the wound bled freely." Later, "A dispatch was sent to the commanding general to announce formally his disability—tidings General Lee had received during the night with profound grief. There came back the following note: 'General: I have just received your note, informing me that you were wounded. I cannot express my regret at the occurrence.

Could I have directed events, I should have chosen, for the good of the country, to have been disabled in your stead. I congratulate you upon the victory which is due to your skill and energy.' When this dispatch was handed to me at the tent, and I read it aloud, General Jackson turned his face away and said, 'General Lee is very kind, but he should give the praise to God.'"

Confederacy, and President Jefferson Davis proclaimed a national day of mourning. Wrote the Sandersville *Central Georgian*, "From the Rio grande to the Potomac will go up one wild wail of lamentation over the great departed. All Israel [the Confederacy] will mourn, for truly a great and good man has fallen."

A hero was dead. The legend that had been born at the Battle of First Bull Run, July 21, 1861, when Thomas Jonathan Jackson earned his nickname, was just beginning.

Mourning women gather around Jackson's grave at the Virginia Military Institute.

The Battle for Vicksburg:

War on the Big River • May 19 – July 4, 1863

Vicksburg, Mississippi. A port town high on an eastern bluff overlooking the mighty river. Its residents regarded it as a place of culture and proudly called it the "Queen City of the Bluff." Lincoln called it simply "the key." He believed its capture was vital to a Northern victory. Controlling Vicksburg meant controlling river traffic. The North had captured New Orleans to the south and had a firm grip north of Memphis, Tennessee. But the middle Mississippi was in Confederate hands. In addition to river traffic, Vicksburg was important as a transfer point for rail and river shipments eastward to the heart of the Confederacy. With New Orleans gone, it became an alternate route for goods shipped to the eastern southland from Texas. Cargo was sent down the Red River, across Louisiana to the Mississippi, and then north about 200 miles to Vicksburg. Southern control of the city also cut off cargo shipments from the midwestern states of the North to New Orleans.

Deciding that Vicksburg must be captured was the easy part. Doing it was another matter. But it wasn't for lack of trying. In early 1862, when Admiral Farragut set sail for New Orleans, he carried orders to take Vicksburg as well.

After the capture of New Orleans on April 25, 1862, had Farragut sailed right up the Mississippi, he might have taken

Vicksburg. Except for its splendid location, it was largely undefended. But many of Farragut's ships had been damaged in the New Orleans battle, and he spent two weeks repairing and resupplying them.

By then it was too late. The fall of New Orleans had sent the Confederacy into a flurry of action. By the time Farragut headed upriver, some 3,500 men in Southern gray had arrived in Vicksburg with more on the way. Heavy guns were installed along the bluffs. Even so, fresh from his victory, Admiral Farragut sailed for Vicksburg with confidence. Farragut had a reputation as a good officer who was somewhat inclined to testiness when things did not go his way. His gruffness, however, was offset by a fine sense of humor. He would need it.

There was trouble right away. Farragut's fleet was meant for the sea, not the Mississippi River. The narrow, twisting, and muddy river channels require flat-bottomed, shallow-draft vessels. Consequently, Farragut's navy constantly ran aground, slowing down the whole operation and bringing misery to the 1,400 soldiers aboard who were meant to be the occupation force after Vicksburg was captured.

But not all was bad news for the admiral. Baton Rouge, the Louisiana capital, surrendered without bloodshed. So did Natchez, Mississippi, where the town citizens dressed up in their finery to see the fleet go by. The richest of Mississippi's planters lived in Natchez, and the good citizens saved the great antebellum houses of the city by surrendering.

Farragut's good humor and confidence were restored as his ships neared Vicksburg. He sent Commander Samuel Phillips Lee, aboard the sloop *Oneida*, to demand the city's surrender. The admiral was in for a shock. Five hours later, he received a reply from Vicksburg's military commander, Colonel James L. Autrey. It said, "Mississippians don't know, and refuse to learn,

VICKSBURG IS THE KEY

No one knew better than President Lincoln how vital the city of Vicksburg was to the war. As a young man, he had worked the riverboats along the wide and twisting curves of the Mississippi. "We can take all the northern ports of the Confederacy," he said, "and they can still defy us from Vicksburg. It means hog and hominy without limit, fresh troops from the States of the far south, and a cotton country where they can raise the staple without interference."

The 1862 efforts of the U.S. Navy helped to prepare the way for Grant's capture of Vicksburg the following year.

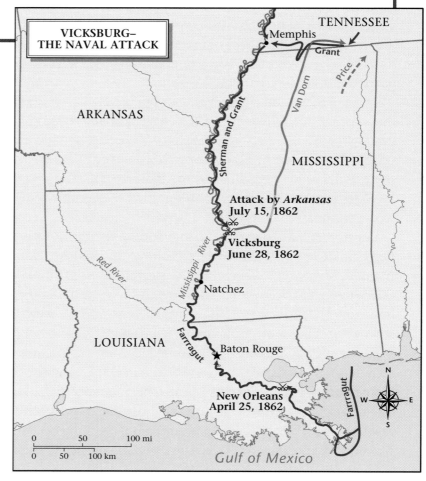

VICKSBURG–
THE NAVAL ATTACK

TENNESSEE
Memphis
Grant

ARKANSAS

Van Dorn

Price

Sherman and Grant

MISSISSIPPI

**Attack by *Arkansas*
July 15, 1862**

Mississippi River

**Vicksburg
June 28, 1862**

Natchez

Red River

LOUISIANA

Farragut

Baton Rouge

**New Orleans
April 25, 1862**

Farragut

0   50   100 mi
0   50   100 km

Gulf of Mexico

N
W   E
S

how to surrender." In other words, he was not going to give up that easily.

Farragut was amazed. Perhaps he had been falsely lulled by the ease of taking Baton Rouge and Natchez. And now what was he to do? The enemy's guns could easily fire down on his ships, but the firepower of his own vessels could not reach the bluffs. He had only 1,400 soldiers on board—most of them seasick—against Confederate troops rumored now to be in the thousands. A cautious man, Farragut sailed back to New Orleans.

President Lincoln, to say the least, was not happy, mostly because the admiral hadn't even fired a gun at the city. Farragut was ordered back to Vicksburg. He set out on June 6, 1862, arriving 19 days later, this time with 3,200 troops and some ships that could lob mortar shells up to the bluffs. That is exactly what they did for two days. Then, Farragut attempted to run by the enemy's batteries with his gunboats. He was fairly successful, with none of the 11 ships suffering serious damage and only 15 Federal sailors lost. But it was a hollow victory. The city was still in Confederate hands. No damage had been done to the powerful Rebel batteries overlooking the river from the bluffs.

Convinced now that Vicksburg could not be taken with a land force of less than 15,000 troops, Admiral Farragut was in for one more nasty surprise. On July 15, his fleet was anchored north of Vicksburg. The admiral, still in his nightshirt, was astounded when the Confederate ship *Arkansas* suddenly swept into view. The *Arkansas*, under command of Lieutenant Isaac Newton Brown, was little more than an amazing collection of railroad irons bolted to a wooden frame and powered by a steamboat engine. This homemade war machine was a fearsome, if strange sight. It was also powerful. The *Arkansas* scored a hit on all of Farragut's wooden ships, killing 12 men and wounding 18.

Humiliated, Farragut vowed revenge. On July 22, he sent two

gunboats against the *Arkansas*. All three ships suffered damage and casualties, but the Confederate's unlikely war vessel survived. However, two days later, when it was feared that the ship would be captured by the North, the *Arkansas* was deliberately destroyed by its own crew.

Farragut sailed back downriver, and the fight for the city on the bluffs was over—temporarily. But 10 months later, President Lincoln was still looking for a way to capture Vicksburg.

The Vicksburg problem wasn't only how to do it, but who to do it. Lincoln's top generals had, by and large, failed him—Hooker at Chancellorsville, Burnside at Fredericksburg; before them, John Pope at Second Bull Run, George McClellan at Antietam, Irvin McDowell at First Bull Run. Lincoln felt that the North had the troops to do the job, but not someone who knew how to use them. "No general yet found," he said, "can face the arithmetic, but the end of the war will be at hand when he shall be discovered."

Of course, there was Ulysses S. Grant, Major General, Army of the Tennessee. The verdict was still out on him, and his record was far from spotless. Grant was 41 years old in 1863. A civilian and a store clerk at the start of the war, he was now commander of the Army of the Tennessee. He had been hailed for his victories at Fort Henry on the Tennessee River and Fort Donelson on the Cumberland in early 1862. At first praised for his bravery at bloody Shiloh that April, he was later criticized for slowness in attacking.

A CITY ATTACKED

Farragut's "run past" Vicksburg on June 18, 1862, whether intended to or not, dropped a heavy load of shells into the city and onto the citizenry. This was the first time in the Civil War that a civilian population had been subjected to a heavy bombardment. The effect was numbing. Men, women, and children fled into the streets in terror as the walls of their homes came crashing down around them. The first private citizen of Vicksburg to die in this bombardment was Mrs. Alice Gamble, who was struck by a shell fragment.

Always a heavy drinker, he was accused, falsely as it turned out, of often being drunk when he should have been leading his men. In addition, he was disliked by his superior, Major General Henry W. Halleck, some said out of jealousy. At any rate, after Shiloh, Halleck in effect took over the Army of the Tennessee, causing Grant to consider resigning his commission. His friend, Major General William Tecumseh Sherman, also at Shiloh, talked him out of it.

That July, Halleck was called to Washington for a new position, general in chief of the Federal Army. He left Grant in charge of the Army of the Tennessee, but cut it in half, both in area and troop strength. Now, Grant had about 100,000 men to protect the southwestern corner of Tennessee. Under his orders, Union troops led by General Rosecrans were victorious at Iuka and Corinth, Mississippi, thus ending Confederate hopes for an invasion of Kentucky.

In the late autumn of 1862, President Lincoln gave Grant the unenviable task of taking Vicksburg. Grant sent General Sherman and 30,000 men down the Mississippi to land just north of Vicksburg at a place called Chickasaw Bluffs. The success of the plan depended on surprise, but neither Sherman nor Grant knew that the Rebels had installed a private telegraph wire along the river and were watching for just such an invasion. When Sherman's forces were spotted, Vicksburg was warned. Without the element of surprise, the Federal troops were driven back from Chickasaw Bluffs on December 29. Another failure, and Vicksburg was still in Confederate hands. Sherman had failed and Farragut before him. But the President wanted the capture of Vicksburg, and now it was up to Grant.

The new year did not look promising. From January through March of 1863, Grant and some 45,000 troops, north of Vicksburg on the other side of Mississippi, tried their best to cross the river.

Nothing worked. The heavy winter rains made movement almost impossible, and any attempt to launch boats was thwarted by the Confederate guns high on the bluffs above the city.

Grant's inability to move his army was getting him some bad publicity back in Washington. Newspaper stories hinted that perhaps the general was drinking again, or just wasn't smart enough to get the job done.

Frustrated and impatient, Grant decided on a new and daring plan. In a report to the President, newspaper editor Charles A. Dana had commented that Grant was "not an original or brilliant man." In fact, as a commander and strategist, Grant was often brilliant and an original thinker. Now, he decided that he would march his troops downriver, cross over below Vicksburg, come up from below the city, and capture it. Even his friend Sherman, a man of no little courage himself, thought he was crazy. Once Grant crossed the Mississippi below Vicksburg, he would be in enemy territory without hope of supply lines or reinforcements. It was a gamble, but, in this instance anyway, Grant was a gambling man.

Once Grant's troops were downriver, they would need boats to

A Confederate officer made this drawing of Admiral Porter's gunboats passing Vicksburg on the night of April 16, 1863.

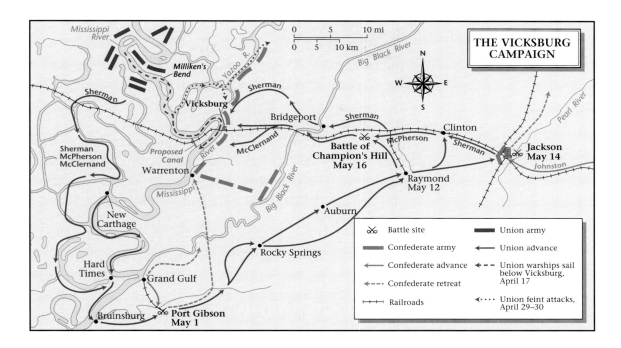

cross the Mississippi. And so, on April 16, 1863, while Sherman drew the Rebels' attention with an attack north of the city, Rear Admiral David Porter and 12 gunboats attempted to blast their way past Vicksburg and its powerful batteries. All but one got through the barrage safely. On April 30, they met Grant and his army and began to ferry them across the Mississippi to Bruinsburg.

Over the next three weeks, Grant conducted what has been called one of the greatest campaigns in military history. In his march to Vicksburg, the city on the bluff, which he reached on May 18, 1863, he marched himself into a long line of military heroes. Cut off from all communication with Washington and with his own supply lines, Grant took his army 180 miles to the northeast, capturing Port Gibson, Raymond, the Mississippi capital of Jackson, and Champion's Hill along the way. In so doing, he outmaneuvered one of the Confederacy's leading generals, Joseph E. Johnston.

After successfully crossing the Mississippi and winning five battles with Confederate forces over a three-week period, Grant was in position to lay siege to Vicksburg.

By Sunday, May 17, Grant's army attacked Confederate forces at Big Black River, just a few miles from Vicksburg. The Confederates, led by Lieutenant General John C. Pemberton, who had stopped Sherman cold at Chickasaw Bluffs, fought with their backs to the river. In danger of being overtaken, they crossed the river to Vicksburg and burned the bridges. Thus Grant's advance was temporarily halted. Even so, General Sherman declared this to be "the end of one of the greatest campaigns in history."

But Vicksburg was still in enemy hands. On May 19, the siege began. After the first attack, Grant's army was repulsed. Wrote a Mississippi chaplain, "Thanks to the great Ruler of the Universe, Vicksburg is still safe."

After two more attacks failed, Grant decided to settle in and outcamp the enemy. His soldiers were happy for the rest and content with the steady barrage of Federal artillery that pounded the area. The citizens of Vicksburg, however, were growing uneasy and frightened. They had been stunned by the news of the defeat at Big Black River and even more so by the presence of the enemy so close to the city. As more and more bedraggled soldiers entered Vicksburg from the defeat at Big Black, their terror grew. It was, perhaps, easy to blame General Pemberton for what seemed certain disaster.

Pemberton, with a force of about 30,000 men, was desperately trying to save the city. He had been urged by Johnston to get his men out of Vicksburg before Grant's troops arrived, but had decided to hold on as long as possible.

In Enemy Country

"A degree of relief scarcely ever equalled since" was how General Grant described his feelings after crossing the Mississippi. "I was now in the enemy's country, with a river and the stronghold of Vicksburg between me and my base of supplies. But I was on dry ground on the same side of the river with the enemy."

MEDAL OF HONOR WINNERS

Medal of Honor winner Orion Howe, of the 55th Illinois, was a 14-year-old drummer boy in the march to Vicksburg. When ammunition ran low, he volunteered to get some. Cautioned that he had to return with .54 caliber only, Howe ran through a hail of musket balls. When he was struck in the leg and taken off to a hospital, he called out to the next messenger, ".54 caliber only!"

Another hero was Private Thomas H. Higgins, who endured a savage onslaught by the soldiers of 2nd Texas and emerged from the dust of battle carrying the U.S. flag. Despite the fierce shooting, he doggedly stepped over fallen bodies and headed for the enemy's lines. "On, you brave Yank!" shouted his fellow soldiers. "Don't shoot that man!" yelled some of the Texans, astonished at his courage. Higgins carried the flag right up to the enemy and was promptly captured. However, his bravado was later rewarded with the Medal of Honor, partly due to testimony given by the enemy.

In the meantime, President Davis hastily called General Lee to Richmond. How could Vicksburg be saved and Grant defeated? Lee proposed a plan. His Army of Northern Virginia would strike into Pennsylvania at Harrisburg and Philadelphia. This would force Grant to take his troops from Vicksburg to defend the Federal capital of Washington. Davis consented and Lee, with 70,000 troops, moved north.

Throughout the month of June, as Lee marched forward to Gettysburg and one of the most important battles of his distinguished career, Grant tightened his hold on the city of Vicksburg. By odd chance, these two most famous generals of the Civil War would suffer significant defeat and victory on different battlefields at just about the same time.

Day after day Yankee artillery pounded Vicksburg, while the Union gunboats shelled from the river. Although only about a dozen citizens were killed during this period, the shelling had great psychological effect. Trails of fire lit up the skies at night, and the people of Vicksburg began to feel as though they were cut off from the rest of the world, as indeed they were. Food ran low. Birds, rats, and squirrels were made into soup. People dug caves in the hillsides to escape the constant shelling. Most of the houses were damaged, and somehow the bombardment sent hundreds of snakes crawling about the streets and lawns.

Yet, despite all this shelling, there was actually little for soldiers and civilians alike to do as they waited for possible surrender. Supposedly, the boredom even got to General Grant, and it is said that once or twice he had to be restrained from appearing before his men in a drunken state.

Still, the city held out. But the end was near, even though the newspaper remained defiant. Wrote the Vicksburg *Citizen,* "The Great Ulysses...has expressed his intention of dining in Vicksburg on the Fourth of July.... Ulysses must get into the city before he dines in it. The way to cook a rabbit is 'first catch the rabbit.'"

Nonetheless, the "Great Ulysses" would have his wish, and General Pemberton knew it. "Proud as I was of my brave troops," he later explained, "honoring them as I did, I felt that it would be

A Brave Youth

One of the Union soldiers wounded at Big Black River was Fred Grant, the general's 12-year-old son. The elder Grant was unaware that the boy had talked himself aboard one of the transports until he was discovered during the landing at Bruinsburg. His bravery was unquestioned, but his youth might account for his reply after being shot in the leg. When asked his condition, the boy declared, "I am killed."

an act of cruel inhumanity to subject them longer to the terrible ordeal. I saw no advantage to be gained by protracting a hopeless defense, which I knew must be attended with a useless waste of life and blood."

On July 3, 1863, while the battle was still in doubt at Gettysburg, Pemberton sent a white flag to the Federal lines. Grant answered with terms of "unconditional surrender." Pemberton refused. The surrender would be conditional, or it would not be at all. Grant accepted the terms that allowed some of the Rebel soldiers to return to their homes. The siege of Vicksburg had lasted 48 days. On July 4, the proud city—with about 30,000 troops—surrendered to the North, and the Civil War had taken one giant step toward a Union victory.

Grant was criticized by his superior, Halleck, for not taking all of the defeated army as prisoners of war. But Grant felt that 30,000 prisoners were enough. Nor did the Northern troops taunt their captured counterparts. A Southerner remarked that the reason was because the Yankees "knew that we surrendered to famine, not to them."

The Stars and Stripes now flew over the courthouse, and Vicksburg citizens came out of their caves and homes to view the destruction. The city did not celebrate another Fourth of July until 1944.

The fight at Gettysburg would become the most talked about and remembered great battle of the war, but the siege of Vicksburg

During the siege of Vicksburg, Union soldiers dug bomb-shelters in the hillside as protection from exploding artillery shells.

African Americans celebrate the arrival of Admiral Porter's fleet and the surrender of Vicksburg.

was probably more important to the outcome. It cut the Confederacy in two. The mighty Mississippi became a Northern highway and when, several days later, Port Hudson, above Baton Rouge, surrendered, Federal ships could sail freely to the sea.

While Southern leaders observed the fall of Vicksburg with the observation that "the Confederacy totters to its destruction," the news brought riotous celebrations in the North. A few days after the victory, President Lincoln sent Grant an extraordinary letter. It said in part, "My Dear General, I do not remember that you and I ever met personally. I write this now as a grateful acknowledgement for the almost inestimable service you have done the country .... When you first reached the vicinity of Vicksburg, ... I never had any faith, except a general hope that you knew better than I ... that the ... expedition and the like could succeed.... and when you turned northward, east of the Big Black, I feared it was a mistake. I now wish to make a personal acknowledgement that you were right and I was wrong."

Was it possible that at long last Lincoln had found his winning general?

Gettysburg:

And the Earth Shook
July 1 - 4, 1863

Wars have a way of putting interesting, perhaps, but otherwise forgettable names into history books. There was Lexington and Concord during the American Revolution. French emperor Napoleon I met his match at Waterloo. World War I had Verdun and the battle of the Argonne Forest. World War II was awash with such places as Dunkirk and Anzio and El Alamein. And for the Civil War, there was Gettysburg. Perhaps no name brings this conflict to mind as does the small village in southern Pennsylvania once called Gettys-town and now the site of a national military park and cemetery. Covering three days, July 1–3, 1863, the Battle of Gettysburg was the greatest ever fought on North American soil, the major conflict of the American Civil War, and generally regarded as its turning point.

Little Gettysburg, the site of Lutheran Theological Seminary (1826) and Gettysburg College (1832), was not the planned meeting place between the Army of the Potomac and the Army of Northern Virginia. Rather, the battle was fought there almost by accident. But once begun, it took on a desperate and terrible life of its own. On 25 miles of Pennsylvania countryside, 160,000 soldiers battled to a degree of violence not seen before or since on American soil. This was Lee's gamble. This was the victory that would turn the tide for the Confederacy. When it did not, the chance had passed. It would not come again.

While General U.S. Grant was threatening Vicksburg in late June 1863, General Lee was marching his troops through Maryland and into Pennsylvania. He was looking for a decisive victory that would swing the war in the Confederacy's favor and he was looking to draw Grant's army away from Vicksburg.

Lee had about 70,000 men under his command, divided into three corps. The 1st was led by Lieutenant General James Longstreet, who had fought at Bull Run, Antietam, and Fredericksburg. Lee called him "my old warhorse" and his men fondly referred to him as "Old Pete." The 2nd Corps, formerly led by Stonewall Jackson, was now commanded by Lieutenant General Richard S. Ewell, who had lost a leg at Second Bull Run. A newly appointed commander, Lieutenant General A.P. (for Ambrose Powell) Hill, led the 3rd Corps.

Union leaders were, of course, not unaware that Lee was heading north. Especially attentive was Major General "Fighting Joe" Hooker, who suggested that with Richmond now largely undefended, this was the perfect time to capture it. But President Lincoln and his general in chief of the Union armies, Henry Halleck, were not confident about Hooker since his defeat at Chancellorsville that May. So, Hooker was told to stay on the defensive and follow Lee wherever he went. Hooker did so, carefully keeping his army between Lee's troops and Washington in case they turned toward the capital.

DANDY JEB

On his way to Gettysburg, General Lee arrived at a railroad whistle-stop one June morning in 1863 to be greeted by his chief of cavalry, Major General Jeb Stuart. Sitting on his flower-bedecked horse, dandy Jeb wore a brand-new uniform with a slouch hat that featured a long, black ostrich plume. Lee was much amused. He later wrote to his wife, "Stuart was in all his glory."

Major General Jeb Stuart

The Union didn't know where Lee was going. Lee didn't know where the Union army was. Between the two, cavalry units dashed back and forth trying to get information or confuse the enemy. One of the units was led by James Ewell Brown Stuart, known as Jeb. Lee called him the "eyes and ears of my army." As such, Stuart came up with an inspired plan. Unfortunately, it helped the other side.

Stuart and his cavalrymen had been camped along the Rappahannock River at Brandy Station, near Culpepper, Virginia. Their mission was, indeed, to be Lee's eyes and ears, to find out what the enemy was doing. Instead, a Union cavalry unit under Alfred Pleasonton surprised Stuart's corps. On June 9, 1863, in the biggest cavalry battle in American history, 21,000 mounted men fought for 12 hours to a standoff.

Jeb Stuart was embarrassed. He was also criticized. The Richmond *Examiner* claimed the surprise attack was brought about by "vain and empty-headed officers." The Richmond *Sentinel* mused that perhaps all should learn a lesson from this, "from the Major General on down." These reports were greeted in Washington by the thought that the proud Stuart would have to do something to restore his reputation.

The major general did not disappoint. Stuart proposed that he could best keep Lee informed of the Union army's movements by riding all the way around it. But Hooker's troops took up far more territory and were moving around far more than Stuart had thought. As a consequence, instead of being Lee's eyes and ears, the chief cavalry unit was totally out of contact with the Confederate army for more than a week. As far as Lee was concerned, Stuart might as well have been on the moon. He would not join Lee until the Battle of Gettysburg was in its second day.

Meanwhile, General Hooker may have been dogging Lee's army, but he was not a happy man. Throughout the month of

June, he had seemed to be walking in a fog. Even his staff officers later said he was entirely at a loss about what to do concerning the enemy. And in a statement not likely to inspire confidence, Hooker complained, "I don't know whether I am standing on my head or feet." Turned down on his request to move on Richmond, he asked for an additional 10,000 men to strengthen his forces. General Halleck turned him down on that, too. Perhaps thinking he could force Washington into giving in to his demands, Hooker asked to be relieved of command. Instead, he gave the President a diplomatic way to change generals. Hooker's resignation was "regretfully" accepted.

But once again, Lincoln needed a commander. On June 28, practically on the eve of the great battle, Major General George Gordon Meade was put in charge of the Army of the Potomac.

Meade was a bookish fellow and a blunt talker, born in Spain and raised in Pennsylvania. He would be defending his home turf at Gettysburg. A veteran of Second Bull Run, Antietam, Fredericksburg, and Chancellorsville, he was steady and solid, if unspectacular. One of his men called him—we do not know if fondly or not—"an old goggle-eyed snapping turtle."

At the time of his unexpected promotion, Meade was in charge of a corps in Hooker's army. A colonel on the War Office staff reached his tent about 3 a.m. on the morning of June 28. Rudely awakened, Meade for a moment thought that he was being arrested for some reason. When he was told the truth, he tried to refuse, claiming that others were more qualified. But it was no use. Meade now headed the Army of the Potomac, like it or not.

And he didn't like it all. For one thing, Hooker had left Meade with no plan for halting Lee's advance and no precise idea of where his army was. Yet, this sort of situation was just what Meade could handle. A graduate of West Point and an engineer, quiet, tall, and balding, Meade was also precise, tough, and reliable. Moreover, he

WILLING OR NOT, HERE I COME

One can suppose that General George Meade was not thrilled to have been given command of the Union Army before Gettysburg. When he heard of his appointment, he said,

"Well, I've been tried and convicted without a hearing. I suppose I shall have to go to execution."

had a hair-trigger temper. By that evening, he had figured out where all his forces were and had decided on a plan. He would move toward the Susquehanna River, which flows from southwestern Pennsylvania into Maryland, keep Washington and Baltimore covered, and if Lee were to move toward Baltimore, would engage him in battle.

General George Meade (fourth from right) and his staff pose for a group photograph.

Meanwhile, without word from Jeb Stuart, Lee was in the dark about where the Union army was and what it was doing. He was quite surprised to learn from a spy that the Federals were now north of the Potomac. He had expected that Stuart would have notified him if the Yanks had moved, but, of course, Stuart was not within communicating distance. Almost incidentially, the spy also told Lee that the Army of the Potomac had a new commander. No one knew much about him.

With the Union troops unexpectedly so close, Lee hastened to pull in his three corps, which were widely separated. The nearest spot for their meeting seemed to be a little crossroads called Gettysburg.

This greatest battle ever fought in North America might be said to have begun over shoes. Word got around that a large supply of shoes was stored at Gettysburg. The Army of Northern Virginia was in very short supply, so about 5:30 a.m., July 1, 1863, some men of Lee's 2nd Corps neared the little town looking for the hidden shoes. Instead, they ran smack into a Union patrol from General John Buford's cavalry unit. This skirmish between a few men on each side would explode into a three-day battle involving some 70,000 men in gray and about 90,000 men in blue. While both sides sent runners in a mad dash to find their armies, the Battle of Gettysburg began.

First Day, July 1: Confederate troops were closer to Gettysburg and got there first. But neither side was really prepared for battle. Lee was unsure of the strength of the Union Army. His 2nd Corps, under General Ewell, was a few hours march away to the north, and Longstreet's 1st Corps was farther to the west. As for Meade, he directed a defensive line to be laid out 20 miles to the southeast. But fighting had already begun in the ridges west of the little town.

The Federals were badly outnumbered on this first day of fighting. Most of their forces had not yet arrived. During a nine-hour desperate fight, some 28,000 Confederate troops battled 18,000 Union soldiers. Central to the battle was the Union infantry corps under command of one of the North's most able leaders, Major General John F. Reynolds. It was Reynolds, along with General Buford, who made the decision that morning to face Lee's army at Gettysburg instead of pulling back to regroup. Buford was watching the Confederates advance from his observation post at the Lutheran Seminary building when Reynolds rode up and asked if his men could hold their position. Buford, a man of few words, said simply, "I reckon I can."

Reynolds, a West Pointer with a crisp professional air who was well liked by his colleagues, was only slightly more talkative than Buford. His message to Meade said, "The enemy is advancing in strong force. I will fight him inch by inch, and if driven into the town I will barricade the streets and hold him back as long as possible."

As a Pennsylvanian, Reynolds was especially determined to keep Gettysburg from the Rebels. He paid for that decision with his life. In midmorning, he took a shell behind the right ear and fell dead from his horse. That left Abner Doubleday, who had been at Fort Sumter when the war began and had fought at Second Bull Run, Antietam, Fredericksburg, and Chancellorsville, in command.

By the afternoon, it was becoming clear that the Union army could not hold out against such overwhelming odds. Slowly they were pushed back through the town at tremendous cost. The 16th Maine, for instance, acting as rear guard, lost 232 of its 298 men. Now watching the retreat was a gray-haired bearded general astride a great gray horse. Robert E. Lee had arrived on the battlefield at Gettysburg with his majestic mount, Traveller.

Late in the afternoon, the Federals were in full retreat, heading south of the town toward the high ground of Cemetery Hill. Interestingly enough, a sign over the small graveyard said, "All persons found using firearms in these grounds will be prosecuted with the utmost rigor of the law."

AN UNEXPECTED MEETING

Major General Abner Doubleday, whose name is forever—rightly or wrongly—linked with baseball, may have been an able soldier, but he seems to have been a courteous, if unthinking, opponent. On the first day of fighting at Gettysburg, his men captured some Rebel soldiers, among them James Archer, whom Doubleday had known before the war. When Archer was brought before him, Doubleday said, "Good morning, Archer, I am glad to see you." Replied an understandably testy Archer, "Well, I am not glad to see you by a darned sight!"

Meanwhile, Lee had stopped on Seminary Ridge, to the left of Cemetery Hill, to watch the Union retreat. Not wanting the enemy to gain the advantage of high ground, he urged Hill and the 3rd Corps to attack. But Hill argued that his men were exhausted and nearly out of ammunition. So, Lee sent a verbal order to Ewell and the 2nd Corps. The order said that Ewell should attack "if he thought it practicable."

It was now about 5:30 in the afternoon. Longstreet arrived with his 1st Corps and urged Lee to move the Confederate forces at once so that they stood between the Federals and Washington, D.C. He felt that the Yanks would see this threat to their capital and would come down the hill after them. But Lee disagreed. "The enemy is there," he said, nodding toward Cemetery Hill, "and I am going to attack him there."

When no answer or action came from Ewell and the 2nd Corps, Lee rode off to find them. General Ewell had already had a bad day. During the fight, he had been shot in the leg. When his officers expressed concern, Ewell assured them he felt no pain. It turns out that the shell had pierced his wooden leg. When Lee

A STAGGERING PRICE

The fighting on the first day of the Battle of Gettysburg ended in a Confederate victory with the Northern troops forced from positions north and west of Gettysburg to the south of the town. A terrible price was paid by both sides. Some of the battle statistics of the dead, wounded, or missing are shocking. For example, the 16th North Carolina lost 75 percent of its 800 men, and the 24th Michigan lost 397 out of 496.

arrived, Ewell explained that it "hadn't been practicable" to attack Cemetery Hill because his men were exhausted and needed the rest.

By that time, it was nearing darkness anyway. The Union army was pouring its strength onto Cemetery Hill and Ridge. The Confederate advantage, for that day, was lost.

On the other side, General Meade was having his own problems. Should he draw his men back to the defensive line he had planned? Should he stay where he was? By midnight, he had made up his mind. Calling his officers to a meeting on Cemetery Hill, he asked for their opinions about where to fight. When they proposed staying where they were, Meade replied, "I am glad to hear you say so, gentlemen. I have already ordered the other corps to concentrate here—and it is too late to change."

Second day, July 2: The sun rose on a warm, sultry July 2nd over the little town of Gettysburg. Throughout the night, troops on both sides had been gathering. The Federals were strung out in a fishhook-like shape running northward for about two miles from the hills of Big Round Top and Little Round Top, along Cemetery Ridge to Cemetery Hill and nearby Culp's Hill. The Confederates were to the left, along the somewhat lower Seminary Ridge. Between the Blue and the Gray lay the battlefield of Gettysburg.

Both generals gave their orders. Take the heights, demanded Lee. Meade, on the job for only five days, was no less firm. His men would, at all costs, hold their ground. "Corps and other commanders are authorized to order the instant death of any soldier who fails in his duty at this hour," he said.

Lee ordered Longstreet and the 1st Corps to take the Round Tops, with Ewell driving on Cemetery and Culp's hills. Longstreet was not happy and protested. He still thought it would be better to swing around the enemy's left, but Lee

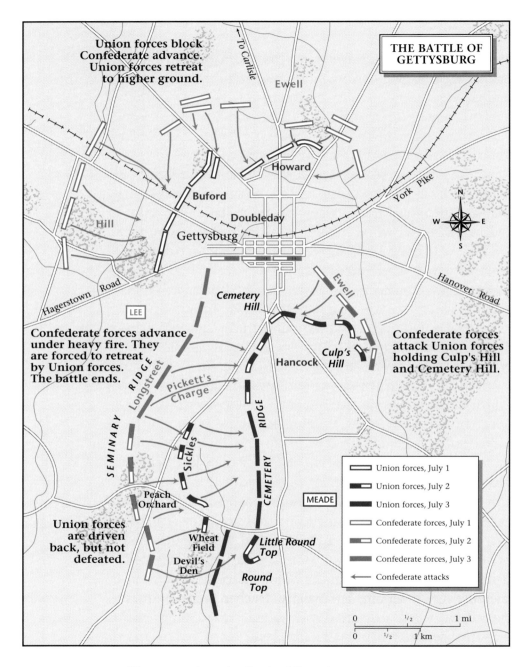

Union forces block Confederate advance. Union forces retreat to higher ground.

THE BATTLE OF GETTYSBURG

To Carlisle

Ewell

Howard

York Pike

Buford

Doubleday

N
W · E
S

Gettysburg

Hill

Hagerstown Road

Hanover Road

LEE

Cemetery Hill

Ewell

Culp's Hill

Confederate forces advance under heavy fire. They are forced to retreat by Union forces. The battle ends.

RIDGE
Longstreet

Pickett's Charge

Hancock

Confederate forces attack Union forces holding Culp's Hill and Cemetery Hill.

SEMINARY

RIDGE

Sickles

CEMETERY

MEADE

Peach Orchard

Union forces are driven back, but not defeated.

Wheat Field

Devil's Den

Little Round Top

Round Top

	Union forces, July 1
	Union forces, July 2
	Union forces, July 3
	Confederate forces, July 1
	Confederate forces, July 2
	Confederate forces, July 3
←	Confederate attacks

0 ... 1/2 ... 1 mi
0 ... 1/2 ... 1 km

The savage three-day Battle of Gettysburg was to prove the turning point of the Civil War.

disagreed. Besides, Longstreet was without the division led by Major General George E. Pickett. It would not reach Gettysburg until late afternoon. Complained Longstreet, "I never like to go into battle with one boot off."

As Longstreet and Ewell were preparing to move, up rode the missing Jeb Stuart, dirty and weary but toting along 125 captured wagons and their teams. Red-faced with anger, Lee said, "I have not heard a word from you for days, and you the eyes and ears of my army." After telling Stuart that his wagons were of little use now, Lee softened and asked for his help in the fight. But the cavalry chief and his tired men were not at full fighting strength until the next day.

Defending against Longstreet's assault on the Round Tops was Union General Daniel Sickles. At least, Sickles was supposed to be defending. The general was a somewhat unpredictable fellow. His chief claim to fame so far had been that, when a congressman before the war, he had killed his wife's lover and had gotten off on a plea of temporary insanity. On this morning, Sickles left the Tops undefended and moved his men into the Peach Orchard, where he believed the Confederates would attack.

Luckily for Meade and the Union, General Gouverneur K. Warren, chief engineer, had climbed Little Round Top to see what was happening. What he saw was Longstreet on the move, Sickles in the Peach Orchard, and the Round Tops with no defense. Realizing that if the Union lost the hills, it would likely lose the battle, Warren quickly sent up four regiments. One of them was the 20th Maine, under command of Colonel Joshua Lawrence Chamberlain, a language teacher from Bowdoin College. He was told to hold Little Round Top "at all hazards." And Chamberlain took his orders seriously.

The 20th Maine had just ten minutes to get into position

behind rocks and trees before they were hit with a furious charge—by the 15th Alabama, under command of Colonel William Oates. In moments, the air was thick with the blue-white smoke of rifle fire and the screams and cries of the wounded. The fighting was so intense and close that sometimes the muzzles of opposing guns nearly touched each other.

The battle lasted an hour and half. Five times, the 15th Alabama drove the 20th Maine from the hill. Five times, Chamberlain and his men returned—what was left of them. The 20th Maine lost 130 of its 350 soldiers in the battle of Little Round top. But they held. For his bravery, Chamberlain was later awarded the Congressional Medal of Honor.

While the Union was holding at Little Round Top, Sickles was in great trouble in the Peach Orchard. The Confederates blasted the area so heavily that small branches were ripped from the trees in a cascade of falling leaves and deadly fire. Horses and men dropped to the ground in an unending parade. One of them was General Sickles himself, his leg torn apart by shells. It is said that he was carried from the battlefield, apparently unruffled and "coolly smoking a cigar." It is also said that after his leg was amputated, the eccentric Sickles ordered the bones to be sent to the Army Medical Museum in Washington, D.C., where he occasionally visited them.

The fighting in the Peach Orchard and the nearby Wheat Field was perhaps the most ferocious of the entire battle. A Texas soldier later recalled that the air was so thick with bullets that he could almost catch a hatful. A private from Massachusetts could not forget the awful sound of the fighting, which he called "... a perfect hell on earth, never, perhaps to be equaled, certainly not to be surpassed, not ever to be forgotten in a man's lifetime."

At one point, Federal troops, in their haste to defend the Wheat Field, opened a gap in their lines on Cemetery Ridge. The

Rebels raced forward to fill it. A tiny regiment, the 1st Minnesota, was ordered to stop them. With fixed bayonets, 262 men raced down the hill full tilt at 1,600 Confederate troops. The Southerners were so startled at the sight that they pulled back. The 1st Minnesota closed the break in the line, but at a terrible cost. In less than five minutes, 82 percent of their number were killed or wounded, the highest casualty percentage of any Union regiment in the entire war.

As night fell on bloody Gettysburg, Lee and Meade retired to plan the next day's strategy. The Confederates had taken the Peach Orchard and the Wheat Field, but the Union still held the all important Little and Big Round Tops. The outcome was in doubt. Wrote Gettysburg resident Sallie Broadhead in her diary that night, "Who is victorious, or with whom the advantage rests,

On July 3, Union and Rebel troops turn a once-peaceful wheat field into a savage battleground.

45

went a long way to deciding the outcome of this day. It occurred to Osborn that if the Union guns stopped firing, the Confederates might well think they had been destroyed. Then, the Rebel infantry might be sent out of the woods into the open. In addition, the cease-fire would conserve precious Federal ammunition.

Osborn gave the order. One by one, Union batteries along the Ridge fell silent.

It worked. The Confederates decided that their shelling had knocked out the enemy guns. Pickett rode up to Longstreet and asked, "Shall I advance?" Overcome with emotion for an action he saw as doomed, Longstreet could only nod his head. Pickett handed him a note he had scribbled to his childhood sweetheart, whom he was about to marry. Then he said, "I shall lead my division forward, sir" and left. Astride his horse facing his men, he said in a clear and steady voice, "Charge the enemy and remember old Virginia."

So began Pickett's Charge. The three divisions, their blue and red flags flapping in the breeze, left the protection of the woods in eerie silence. At a steady pace of about 100 yards a minute, they advanced. The sight was almost paralyzing to the enemy waiting on the hills.

Various figures have been given for the number of men in Pickett's Charge. They range from 15,000 to 10,000, with most historians agreeing at

Pickett's Charge. What started as a gallant and orderly advance on Federal troops soon turned into one of the bloodiest and most ghastly scenes of the Civil War.

AWE-INSPIRING IN ITS HORROR

A Union officer watched the approach of Pickett and his men. "More than half a mile their front extends ... man touching man, rank pressing rank ... The red flags wave, their horsemen gallop up and down ... barrel and bayonet gleam in the sun, a sloping forest of flashing steel. Right on they move, as with one soul, in perfect order without impediment of ditch, or wall, or stream, over ridge and slope, through orchard and meadow, and cornfield, magnificent, grim, irresistible."

Said another, "It was the most beautiful thing I ever saw."

In the aftermath of Gettysburg, the dead and mortally wounded of both sides lay strewn over the battlefields.

about 12,500. Whatever the figure, it was certainly awesome.

Pickett's Charge, for all its military drama, was surely doomed from the start. The Confederates had to cross almost a mile of open ground under direct long- and short-range fire. As a Union soldier later said, "We could not help hitting them at every shot." Yet, at one point several hundred Southerners broke through the Union center at what was called the High-Water Mark. Then, the Union line quickly closed.

Late in the day, as charge after charge was driven back by the Federal troops, Lee clung to hope. When he ordered Pickett to prepare his division for a possible counterattack, Pickett replied, "I have no division now." The Confederate infantry suffered a nearly 60 percent casualty rate on that day.

Pickett lost nearly 3,000 of his men in the famous charge, as well as 16 out of 17 of his field officers. He never forgot them and he never forgave Lee for the disaster. Perhaps Lee never forgave himself. As the remains of the defeated Army of Northern Virginia left the battlefield, a sad and weary Robert E. Lee could only say, "All this has been my fault." The Battle of Gettysburg was over. The North had won.

As dawn broke on the Fourth of July 1863, a long wagon train carrying dead and wounded home to the South began its retreat from the fields of Gettysburg. Pelted by heavy rain, the infantry and artillery followed. This major battle of the Civil War was finished. The tide may have turned, but the war was far from over. Meade, so short a time on the job, had acquitted himself well in this terrible battle. Now, he decided not to pursue the defeated Confederates. Instead, he watched them go. The Federal Army in its victory suffered more than 23,000 casualties at Gettysburg. The Confederate Army in its defeat listed 28,000 as dead, wounded, or missing. The fewer than 3,000 citizens of Gettysburg were left with thousands of dead and wounded to attend to. A calm and deliberate Meade decided to rest his army.

Encouraged as he was with the victory, especially as it was coupled with news of Grant's capture of Vicksburg, Lincoln was disappointed with Meade's decision. Another opportunity to destroy the Army of Northern Virginia had been lost.

As for Lee, he wrote a letter to President Davis offering his resignation. Lee had been ill earlier in the year and still felt somewhat feeble. Now, he feared he had lost the confidence of his men. Perhaps a younger and more able commander would better serve the cause. But Davis would not hear of it. To find a better commander than Lee, said the Confederate president, was "an impossibility."

Various reasons have been given for Lee's defeat in this greatest battle of his career. He was ill served by Jeb Stuart and Ewell and hindered by a testy Longstreet, even though his opposition to Pickett's Charge proved correct. Never certain of where the enemy was, Lee felt compelled to make a stand at Gettysburg.

Lee would not mount another full-scale invasion of the North. A precious opportunity had been lost. But Meade's decision to rest his army left the Confederate general to fight another day. And so he would.

After the Battle of Gettysburg, Lee's army, its wagons filled with wounded and its battle-torn flag still flying, begins its retreat to Virginia.

Taking Chattanooga:

From Chickamauga to Missionary Ridge
September to November 1863

The Stars and Stripes fluttered in the summer breezes over Vicksburg, Mississippi. A defeated Army of Northern Virginia slowly retreated from the fields of Gettysburg into Virginia. But President Abraham Lincoln knew the war was far from over. To win it, the North would need more soldiers for the victorious but tired armies of Meade and Grant. He issued a call for 300,000 fresh troops.

On Saturday, July 11, the names of the first draftees appeared in the newspapers. Resentment against the Federal draft had been building and by Monday, New York City was the scene of an out-of-control mob running through the streets in a fury of burning and looting. Often as not, the targets were the homes and buildings of black Americans. About 1,000 people were killed and wounded, with damages running over one million dollars. The New York Draft Riot, which lasted for three days and spread to other cities, was one of the darkest periods of the Northern homefront during the Civil War.

The draft call, which had to be suspended and was not renewed until August 19, included all men between 20 and 45 for an enlistment period of three years. But what caused the resentment was the commutation fee. Quickly known as the "rich man's bill," it allowed any man with $300 to buy his way out of service, or he could pay a substitute to take his place. Quite

naturally, many of the rich did. Future presidents Chester A. Arthur and Grover Cleveland bought substitutes. So did business tycoons J.P. Morgan and Andrew Carnegie. So did the fathers of future presidents Theodore and Franklin Roosevelt. Even Lincoln, trying to set an example, paid someone to take his place, although technically he was too old for military service anyway. His substitute was John Summerfield Staples, from Stroudsburg, Pennsylvania.

Who were the soldiers who made up the armies of the North and South? Generally speaking, they were men who really wanted to go to war—at least in the beginning. For some there was the pure adventure of it. Many young men, both North and South, saw the army as a way to get off the farm and see the nation. And most truly believed in the causes for which they

Police charge a mob armed with bricks, clubs, and rifles during the New York Draft Riot. Workers who feared losing their jobs in the city to an influx of freed slaves were among the angriest demonstrators.

fought. It wasn't long, however, before their illusions of glory were lost on the bloody battlefields. In general, the soldiers of the Blue and Gray were poorly trained, poorly cared for, poorly led, and poorly disciplined. They had to learn the business of war as they went along, if they lived, for there were few qualified to teach them. Most of them never quite got the hang of the strict discipline that is part of today's military machine. They might obey an order and say "yes, sir," but it was apt to be done with an ummistakable air of informality. And with rare exceptions, they never quite mastered the "lockstep" marching so admired in today's military corps.

Not that the Civil War soldier was without discipline at all. Some things were simply not tolerated. Running or hiding from battle was punishable by public humiliation. The soldier had to wear a sign on his back that said "Coward." If he was convicted of drunkenness, the most punished offense, he had to stand on a box for a day or two with a log on his shoulder. And a conviction of desertion, under certain circumstances could mean, then as now, death.

There is probably never a "good" time to go to war and that was certainly true for the Civil War soldier. The killing power on both sides was growing more efficient, which meant that he might be injured quite badly. But his medical care, if it existed at all, was shamefully poor by modern standards.

It was not that either side didn't want to tend their soldiers in the best way possible. The doctors of the time simply did not know how. It occurred to practically no one that a bandage should be "sterilized" before being applied to a wound. Most would not have known what "sterilized" meant. Few doctors did more than "rinse off" their instruments—if they did that—between operations at a field hospital.

And if the Civil War soldier did survive medical treatment, he was quite likely to die in camp anyway of disease, pneumonia, typhoid, or the incredibly unsanitary conditions under which he lived. Although most doctors of the time understood that there was a connection between sanitation and health, few knew what to do about it. If the camp's water supply didn't smell too bad, it was considered safe.

More than a few soldiers on either side owed their lives to the hundreds of volunteers, mostly women but men, too, who tended the sick and wounded in field hospitals. Said one Southern volunteer, "I have never worked so hard in all my life and I would rather do that than anything else in the world."

Two women, Dorothea Dix (1802–1887) and Clara Barton (1821–1912), often called Angels of the Battlefield, were especially known for their tireless efforts in organizing nursing corps. Dix recruited women to serve as nurses in the Army Medical Bureau. After the war, Barton was instrumental in

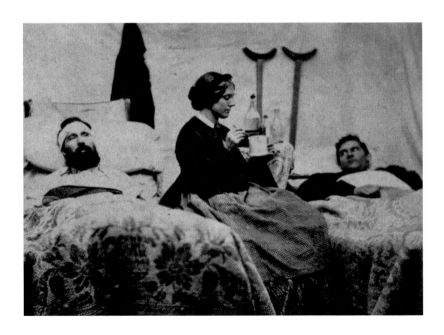

A nurse tends to two wounded men in a Union hospital at Nashville, Tennessee.

A Poet Volunteers

American poet Walt Whitman (1819–1892) served as a hospital nurse in Washington, D.C., during the Civil War. He wrote, "When I go into a new ward, I always carry two or three quires of paper and a good lot of envelopes and walk up and down and circulate them around to those who desire them .... He who goes among the soldiers with gifts, etc., must beware how he proceeds.... They are not charity patients but American young men of pride and independence."

creating an American branch of the International Red Cross.

Poorly trained he may have been and too idealistic at first, but the Civil War soldier became the strongest and bravest of fighting men. He held his fears in check and stood his ground often under the most hopeless of battlefield conditions. His courage was often tested but rarely found wanting.

After Gettysburg, a kind of lull descended on the Civil War. Lee and Meade nursed their wounds. After Vicksburg, Grant wanted to swing on through the South, convinced that no one could stop him. The government in Washington, however, was more interested in occupying Southern territory, so Grant was forced to scatter his troops.

Minor battles were fought throughout the South during the summer months of 1863. In late August, William Clarke Quantrill led Confederate guerrillas in a terrorist attack at Lawrence, Kansas, killing about 150 civilians. As summer gave way to fall, there was still little action in Virginia and the Mississippi valley, but things were heating up in middle Tennessee. The object was the city of Chattanooga, a railroad and industrial center near the border of Georgia on the Tennessee River. If the North had Chattanooga, it could move into Knoxville and eastern Tennessee, which was strongly pro-Union.

But Chattanooga was in the hands of the Confederates, led by General Braxton Bragg, commander of the Army of Tennessee, and about 43,000 men. A commander at the Battle of Shiloh,

Bragg was a sour-faced sort, noted for strict discipline, and generally disliked by his troops who thought he was a tyrant. Nonetheless, they fought for him, and fought well.

During the summer of 1863, Major General William S. Rosecrans of Ohio and his 60,000-strong Army of the Cumberland moved in. Old Rosy, as his men called him, was a well-liked, dependable officer who had led part of Grant's forces at Corinth, Mississippi. Now he executed a series of tricky maneuvers that fooled Bragg and lured his forces out of Chattanooga. The Federals took control without having to fight a battle.

Rosecrans had little time to enjoy his victory, however. Bragg, reinforced with troops from Longstreet's veteran corps, sent by rail from Lee's army in Virginia, now used a little trickery of his own. He lured part of the Union army out of the city and attacked in a vicious two-day battle along Chickamauga Creek, Georgia.

Chickamauga, about 12 miles southeast of Chattanooga, means "river of death" in the Cherokee language. It lived up to its name on September 19 and 20, 1863. The casualty list including wounded for the North totaled about 16,000; for the South, 20,000. In all, 4,000 soldiers died along Chickamauga Creek on those two days.

Bragg had his costly victory. Rosecrans and part of his army fled in disarray back to the city.

A VIRGINIAN FOR THE UNION

Virginia-born Major General George H. (Pap) Thomas paid a high price for staying with the Union during the Civil War. Northern leaders questioned his loyalty, and some members of his family never spoke to him again. Through it all, Thomas remained true to his beliefs. A comrade called him a "model man and true soldier."

Major General "Pap" Thomas

Lincoln later said Rosecrans was "confused and stunned, like a duck hit on the head."

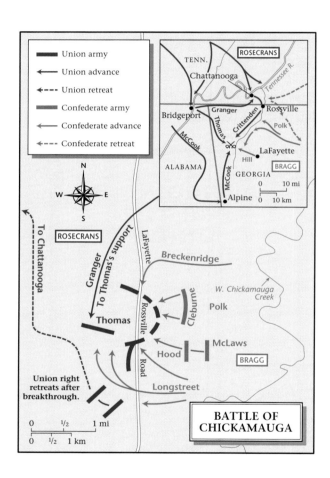

The ferocious Battle of Chickamauga on September 19-20, 1863, resulted in a victory for the South.

The entire Army of the Cumberland might have been wiped out at Chickamauga had it not been for Major General George H. Thomas, known as Pap. His stubborn defensive battle and orderly withdrawal to Chattanooga saved the rest of the Army of the Cumberland and earned Pap the nickname of Rock of Chickamauga.

While Bragg was victorious at Chickamauga Creek, that victory did little for his reputation or career. He refused to follow up his advantage by taking the city. His officers were furious, and Longstreet demanded his removal. "I am convinced," he said, "that nothing but the hand of God can help as long as we have our present commander." Although all the Confederate corps commanders called for Bragg's removal, President Davis, who rarely listened to his officers anyway, refused.

Lincoln was doubly saddened after Chickamauga, by the defeat and by the fact that Confederate Brigadier General Ben Hardin Helm, his wife's brother-in-law, died there. Mary Lincoln, however, had some bitter words. Remarking to a friend that she did not care if all her Confederate relatives were killed, she added, "They would kill my husband if they could, and destroy our Government—the dearest thing of all to us."

The short battle at Chickamauga Creek produced a big change for the North and, eventually, the outcome of the war. Lincoln decided to promote Ulysses S. Grant. On October 17, Grant was named supreme commander of the Federal forces in the West.

Grant hurried to Chattanooga. He replaced Rosecrans with Rock of Chickamauga Thomas. Old Rosy's career as a field commander was ended and he was reassigned to duty in St. Louis.

The Yanks now held Chattanooga, but they were in trouble. Bragg's forces almost encircled the city. Supplies could not get in and the army could not get out, not that any army under Thomas would have been likely to retreat. But when Grant arrived, said an officer, "we began to see things move.... everything came from a plan."

Breaking a hole through the Rebel line, Grant had a pontoon bridge laid across the Tennessee River. This set up a 60-mile so-called "cracker line" to bring in food supplies. The 11th and 12th Corps, under command of Fighting Joe Hooker, were called in from Alabama. They had been earlier sent by rail from Meade's Army of the Potomac.

While the Federal army was making plans to secure Chattanooga, an historical—but at the time little noticed—event was taking place on the now quiet battlefield of Gettysburg. A new Union military cemetery was dedicated there on November 19, 1863. The main attraction was the former governor of Massachusetts, Edward Everett, known for his flowery and patriotic speechmaking. Almost incidentally, President Lincoln had been invited to "make a few remarks."

Everett spoke for nearly two hours. By that time, the 6,000 spectators were somewhat bored and restless. They'd had about all the lemonade and cookies they could consume and had bought all the buttons and dried wildflowers for sale by the local vendors. The President, still fussing with the wording of his remarks a short time earlier, was introduced. He stood, put on his spectacles, and read from a sheet of paper. Lincoln spoke for two minutes. The entire speech consisted of 10 sentences and 271 words. The photographer didn't even have time to take a picture.

When it was over, the spectators said things like "Is that all?" "Did he finish?" No one applauded and most everyone was disappointed. What kind of speech was that from a president?

THE GETTYSBURG ADDRESS

Four score and seven years ago our fathers brought forth on this continent a new nation, conceived in liberty, and dedicated to the proposition that all men are created equal.

Now we are engaged in a great civil war, testing whether that nation, or any nation so conceived and so dedicated, can long endure. We are met on a great battlefield of that war. We have come to dedicate a portion of that field as a final resting place for those who here gave their lives that that nation might live. It is altogether fitting and proper that we should do this.

But, in a larger sense, we can not dedicate— we can not consecrate—we can not hallow— this ground. The brave men, living and dead, who struggled here, have consecrated it, far above our poor power to add or detract. The world will little note, nor long remember, what we say here, but it can never forget what they did here. It is for us the living, rather, to be dedicated here to the unfinished work which they who fought here have thus far so nobly advanced. It is rather for us to be here dedicated to the great task remaining before us—that from these honored dead we take increased devotion to that cause for which they gave the last full measure of devotion—that we here highly resolve that these dead shall not have died in vain—that this nation, under God, shall have a new birth of freedom—and that government of the people, by the people, for the people, shall not perish from the earth.

Most journalists said it was silly and vulgar. The London *Times* pompously said, "Anyone more dull and commonplace it would not be easy to produce." Lincoln himself called it a "flat failure."

But some, just a few, thought the Gettysburg Address was an elegant definition of the ideals that are worth fighting and dying for. Equality is worth fighting for, and freedom for all is worth dying for. Lincoln said that those honored that day at Gettysburg had given their lives for a noble ideal, once again proving that freedom is not free.

Today, Lincoln's short, almost unnoticed speech is one of the nation's most quoted and revered documents and is known around the world. Those few remarks have been called a masterpiece of literature. It is a piece better read than heard to grasp the elegance of its phrasing and the power of its intent.

Four days after the Gettysburg Address, the Battle of Chattanooga began (November 23–25, 1863). Bragg was outnumbered at the start because of his own mistake. He had sent some 12,000 men and more cavalry under Longstreet to Knoxville. A Federal force had come down from the mountains to occupy the city, but at the moment it was of no particular threat to Bragg's army. As a result, his 46,000 men now faced an enemy numbering about 56,000.

Bragg's forces were strung out for six miles along Missionary Ridge east of the city. His guns looked down south and west from 2,000-foot-high Lookout Mountain.

General Thomas opened the battle on November 23 by seizing Orchard Knob, about a mile in front of the Confederate position on Missionary Ridge. The following day, Hooker took three Federal divisions to the top of Lookout Mountain, where they planted the U.S. flag. Actually, it was less of a victory than it looked because, as it turned out, only an enemy skeleton force had been left to guard it. But it was a spectacular victory

This artist's rendition shows Union soldiers, under the command of General Hooker, storming Lookout Mountain on November 24, 1863.

nonethless for the fog was so heavy at that height on that day that the fight is known as the Battle Above the Clouds.

As Hooker battled on Lookout Mountain, General William Sherman, who had been called east from Memphis, was stalled in his attempt to attack the Confederates on Missionary Ridge. He was still stalled on November 25. Grant now urged Thomas to attack the Rebels at the base of the ridge, hoping to draw fire away from Sherman. Thomas did more than that. He was tired of being taunted for the defeat at Chickamauga and tired of being reminded by Sherman and Hooker that he and his men had to be rescued. When General Philip Sheridan, who was with Thomas, became angry when enemy fire dirtied his uniform that seemed to be a signal. As one moving mass, the Union troops—

LIKE FATHER, LIKE SON

Three flag bearers of the 24th Wisconsin were killed while trying to carry the unit's flag up Missionary Ridge through a heavy barrage of fire. The fourth carrier, an 18-year-old lieutenant, was finally successful. He reached the top, shouting, "On, Wisconsin!" His superior recommended Lieutenant Arthur MacArthur, Jr., for the Congressional Medal of Honor, which probably later impressed his own son, General Douglas MacArthur, American hero of World War II.

shouting "Chickamauga! Chickamauga!"—overtook the Rebel positions and stormed right past them up Missionary Ridge. In one burst of anger and energy, they drove Bragg's men off the hill and secured Chattanooga.

It was an important victory for the Federals. They now had Chattanooga and Knoxville. The North had sustained nearly 6,000 casualties, the South about 6,500. The Confederates had lost the war in the West. Bragg and his army withdrew into Georgia. However, Bragg had lost more than Chattanooga. Davis finally gave in to the advice of his generals and accepted Bragg's resignation, replacing him with Joseph E. Johnston.

Besides the North itself, Grant would prove to be the biggest winner at Chattanooga. He was about to get another promotion. For the time being, however, both armies went into winter rest.

Grant and Lee:

The Battles of 1864

5 On March 9, 1864, Ulysses S. Grant was commissioned a lieutenant general. It was a rank Congress re-created for him at Lincoln's request. On March 12, his new job was made public—general in chief of the armies of the United States. He replaced Major General Halleck, who became chief of staff. It had taken a long time, but President Lincoln was now convinced that he had found the right man—a soldier to do a soldier's work. Grant would leave policy to government and devote himself solely to the task of defeating Robert E. Lee and the Confederate Army.

Who were these two imposing figures who had such impact on the outcome of the American Civil War?

There is little about the early years of Hiram Ulysses Grant (1822–1885) to suggest he would amount to much. His father was a tanner in Point Pleasant, Ohio; his grandfather had been in prison for debts. He was short, shy, and withdrawn. By the time his father got him into West Point in 1839, he had reversed his name to Ulysses Hiram. But a clerk at the Point enrolled him as Ulysses Simpson (his mother's maiden name). Not wanting to cause a fuss, he used the name of Ulysses S. Grant for the rest of his life.

Grant was happy at West Point, not because he was fond of the military, but because he was fond of horses. An expert horseman at an early age, he hoped to be assigned to the cavalry. The army chose not to do so. He had not been a distinguished cadet, graduated in the middle of his class, and his friends called him Sam.

Grant fought in the Mexican War because, although he considered it unjust, he also considered it his duty. In 1848, he married Julia Dent, sister of his West Point roommate, and the romance lasted all their lives. They had three sons and a daughter.

When the army sent him west and he had no money to bring his family, Grant was miserable and lonely and began to drink. He resigned his commission in 1854 and rejoined his family back east. Money was always a problem. No matter what he tried failed. He was a clerk in Galena, Illinois, when the Civil War started and he went back into the army.

Grant was not a "spit and polish" sort of soldier. Thick-bodied and stoop-shouldered, he tended to be somewhat untidy in his dress and didn't even like uniforms. He didn't much like marching bands either. In fact, he said he knew only two songs: "One was Yankee Doodle, the other wasn't." He was inclined to become blue and depressed at times, which is when he drank. But he was clearheaded and clearminded under fire and never lost sight of his objective. His loyalty and his bravery were unquestioned. So was his compassion for his men. In battle, he would often spend nights far from the hospital tents so that he would not hear the suffering of the wounded. Yet, he never hesitated to send men into battle, even under challenging odds. He accepted the criticism for losing too many of his soldiers at the Battle of Shiloh (April 1862) in angry silence.

With his commission as lieutenant general, this man who

A brilliant, but not very tidy General Grant (far left) smokes a cigar after the Union victory at Lookout Mountain.

65

A Long Career

Robert E. Lee's long army career began on the day of his West Point graduation in 1829 and ended when he accepted defeat for the Confederacy in 1865. Even in the most difficult of times, Lee, shown here as a young officer, conducted himself with honor and dignity. In his farewell speech to his troops after the surrender, he said, "I have consented to this result...feeling that valor and devotion could accomplish nothing that could compensate for the loss that would have attended the continuation of the contest...I bid you an affectionate farewell."

Robert E. Lee

would become the 18th president of the United States (1869–1877) had only one objective, which he followed singlemindedly until the end of the war: Defeat Lee and the Army of Northern Virginia.

Grant's background was very different from that of the general who opposed him—Robert Edward Lee (1807–1870). Born in Stratford, Virginia, Lee was related to most of the state's most imporarant families. His father, "Light Horse Harry" Lee, had fought in the American Revolution and had been a governor of Virginia. He had also been a spendthrift and something of a hellion. He died when Lee was 11 and his mother raised him as a southern gentleman.

At West Point, Lee was the perfect cadet, receiving not one demerit in all four years. Despite that, his classmates liked him, fondly referring to him as the "Marble Model." He graduated second in his class in 1829. In 1831, he married Mary Custis, granddaughter of Martha Washington.

Lee was as distinguished a soldier as he had been a cadet. In addition, he neither smoked, drank, nor cursed. Lest he sound too perfect, he did have a terrible temper, which he tried to control. And although he was always faithful to his wife, it is said he did realize that women found him attractive as he sat astride his great gray horse called Traveller. Lee did own a few slaves, whom he freed before the war. Still there were many slaves on his wife's plantation.

As brave and honorable on the battlefield as Grant, Lee was

offered command of the United States Army at the start of the war in 1861. Although he had taken an oath to support the U.S. Constitution, he refused. Not particularly pro-slavery (but certainly not opposed to it) or states' rights, Lee was, above all, a Southerner and he felt his duty and his honor were owed to Virginia.

Lee's officers and men loved him. Stonewall Jackson said he would follow him into battle blindfolded. Now Lee would face his greatest test.

In the early months of 1864, the Confederacy was holding its own. Despite fierce naval bombardment of Fort Sumter and Charleston, the Rebel flag still flew over the city. In late February, the North lost battles at Olustee, Florida, and Okolona, Mississippi. Lee and his forces were resting along the Rapidan River in northern Virginia. The Army of Tennessee, now commanded by Joseph E. Johnston, was keeping a watchful eye on the troops assembling around Chattanooga under command of General William Tecumseh Sherman.

Once Grant was given full command, he outlined a plan for the final objective—the defeat of the Confederacy. Since the war began, he said, the Union army, although superior in number, had been divided and acting independently. Now, he would concentrate all Northern forces against the Confederate armies in the field. There were just two armies that concerned him: Lee's incomparable Army of Northern Virginia and Johnston's tested Army of Tennessee. Accordingly, Grant ordered Major General Benjamin F. Butler to lead his troops up the James River in central Virginia toward Richmond. German-born Major General Franz Sigel would march through the Shenandoah Valley in northwestern Virginia, also heading for Richmond. Sherman would leave Chattanooga and strike out for Atlanta, Georgia. General George G. Meade, who was still technically in charge of the Army of the Potomac, would lead his 110,000 men south to face Lee. "Wherever Lee goes, you will go also," Grant said. That meant, so would Grant. For although he was now general in chief, Grant had no plans to remain in Washington. He made his headquarters with the Army of the Potomac and would travel with it.

Grant's mission was simple. All units would move together. Throw everything against the 60,000-man Army of Northern Virginia. When something broke, crash on through and head for the Confederate capital of Richmond, just as Sherman was heading for Atlanta. But Grant was not truly interested in taking Richmond; he was truly interested in defeating Lee.

Camped along the Rapidan River in northern Virginia near a tangled thicket known as the Wilderness, Lee and his army waited. A year before, they had outsmarted the Yanks, then led by Hooker, in this same area. But Longstreet well knew the difference this time. "That man," he said, referring to Grant, "will fight us every day and every hour until the end of the war."

"That man" was at the moment crossing the Rapidan, intent on getting Lee into open country where the superior numbers of the Northern army could be used to full advantage. But Lee had a habit that often proved infuriating to opposing generals. He liked to choose where to fight. So, he ordered his outnumbered army into the Wilderness. Grant would not have his open country.

It was a lovely spring morning on the 5th of May, 1864, when the Battle of the Wilderness began. But the Wilderness was not a lovely place to be, and it was a bad place to fight. The underbrush was so thick that it was difficult to see more than a few yards in any direction. Even that limited visibility was soon lost in a great cloud of smoke and fire. In fact, General Longstreet was wounded in the head and neck by his own men. But the superior numbers of the U.S. Army meant little here. Their superior artillery meant nothing at all because it couldn't be used. Actually, the Confederate soldiers probably had the easier time of it because more of them were used to such country areas.

It was a horrible, vicious, bloody fight that would last for two days. The thick underbrush often caught fire. On the second night, it is reported that Grant wept in his tent as flames swept through the Wilderness, burning alive many of his wounded men.

When the smoke cleared, Grant learned that his list of those killed, wounded, missing, and captured reached 17,000. The Confederates, with about 7,000 casualties, captured two generals and 600 prisoners and nearly cut off Grant's supply lines. Characteristically, Grant remained silent when he heard the news. An officer said that he "... gives no expression of his feelings and no evidence of his intentions. He smokes almost constantly, and ... has a habit of whittling with a small knife. He cuts a small stick into small chips, making nothing."

It looked as though Grant was beaten just about as badly as Hooker had been a year earlier. Yet, there was a vast difference. Grant was not Hooker. And Lee knew it. Said he to his officers, "Grant is not going to retreat."

THE GREAT MOTIVATOR

During the Battle of the Wilderness, Confederate General John Gregg and his Texans were ordered to plug a hole in the lines. "Scarce had we moved a step," remembered Gregg, "when General Lee in front of the whole command, raised himself in his stirrups, uncovered his grey hairs, and with an earnest voice exclaimed ... 'Texans always move them.' Never before in my lifetime did I ever see such a scene as was enacted when Lee pronounced these words. A yell rent the air that must have been heard for miles around. ... A courier riding by my side, with tears coursing down his checks, exclaimed, 'I would charge hell itself for that old man.'"

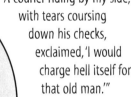

General John Gregg

And, indeed, he did not. When the Army of the Potomac left the Wilderness, it moved south. Grant's men sent up a cheer. For the first time in the war, the Federals did not retreat after losing a battle. With this decisive action, Grant very nearly turned the Wilderness defeat into victory. "Whatever happens," Grant had told Lincoln, "we will not retreat." The North had a new leader, and this was a new war.

Lee judged correctly that Grant would turn south. He also guessed where Grant would go. Right again. On May 7, as Sherman began his long drive toward Atlanta, Grant hurried his army to a crossroads 11 miles south of Fredericksburg, called Spotsylvania Court House.

Lee was waiting. In some of the most ferocious fighting of the war, the two armies clashed for 12 long days, including one solid day of hand-to-hand combat at a spot that earned the name "Bloody Angle." Once again, Grant withdrew and counted his casualties—more than 18,000. About 10,000 Confederates died or were wounded or captured.

For the next several savage and bloody weeks, these two generals and their armies struggled along a 100-mile crest as they traveled south toward Richmond. Again and again, Grant tried to get around the right flank of Lee's army and destroy it. Again and again, the Confederate leader outguessed and outfoxed him. It was a strange deadly dance of tactics and maneuvering. A sidestep here, a dodge there. But always when they met, there were grievous losses—at the North Anna River, May 23–26, and at Totopotomoy Creek. Grant always arrived to find Lee awaiting him. Finally, at Cold Harbor on June 3, 1864, Grant, Meade, and the Army of the Potomac launched a savage, near-suicidal attack in what seemed a desperate effort to break through the Confederate lines. In less than one hour, Grant's casualty list numbered 7,000. Lee, with probable losses of about

1,500, could claim a great victory that day, but it would be his last major triumph in all-out battle.

Grant called off the attack about noon and later regretted ordering it at all. Charles Francis Adams, Jr., of the Army of the Potomac, agreed. He wrote that although he had great faith in Grant, the army "has literally marched in blood and agony from the Rapidan to the James." Others agreed, too. After all, in some 30 days, Grant had lost more than 40,000 men, killed, wounded, or missing. Some began to grumble that he was no better at winning the war than the generals before him. The President's wife actually called him a butcher.

On June 2, 1864, Grant leans over a bench (at left) to study a map with his officers and plan their attack on Cold Harbor the next day.

Grant kept silent and kept going. Like a battered boxer refusing to stay down, he counted his losses, licked his wounds, and got ready for the final assault on Richmond. On June 12, with rapidity and secrecy, he began one of the great army movements in military history. The rail and communications center of Petersburg, south of Richmond, was his objective. If he could take it and block out the Confederate supply lines, Richmond would be forced to surrender. Under cover of darkness, after a fake move toward Richmond, Grant shifted his army toward the James River.

Lee made his first mistake. Judging that Grant would attack

Richmond, he sent most of his army there. Instead, Grant's engineers were building a pontoon bridge across the James River. They did it in eight hours on June 14. By June 16, the massive Army of the Potomac was on the south shore.

The attack on Petersburg began on Wednesday, June 15. It should have worked. The rail center was guarded by none other than P.G.T. Beauregard, the dandy general who had gained fame at Fort Sumter, First Bull Run, and Shiloh. At first, he had only about 3,000 troops against an advance guard of some 16,000, under General W.F. "Baldy" Smith.

But this was not the first time, nor the last, that a battle was lost due to mixups in orders, poor timing, or lack of communication. Reinforcements were late in getting to Smith, who was slow in attacking. Beauregard's defense was unexpectedly strong. Lee discovered Grant's true whereabouts and sent in reserves. Despite repeated assaults, Petersburg held. On June 18, Grant decided the city could not be taken by storm. The four days at Petersburg cost the Union about 8,000 men.

Half the year was gone. Lee had not been defeated. Richmond had not been taken. Nor had Petersburg. Grant decided he must capture Petersburg as he had captured Vicksburg. And so the Army of the Potomac settled down to a nine-month siege of the city.

Back home, no one was happy either. To the North, the war once again seemed at a standstill, except for the growing casualty figures. It was difficult to see what Grant had achieved, if anything. Lincoln's chances for reelection in the fall began to look doubtful.

But if others were not, Lee was well aware of what had been happening. Grant's dogged pursuit of the Confederates had kept them on the defensive, not allowing Lee to pull off one of the dazzling and unexpected strikes for which he was noted. He almost did, however.

In July, Lee sent Lieutenant General Jubal Early and 14,000 men in a dash up the Shenandoah Valley into Maryland. The objectives were to strike terror into Northern citizens, which they did, and to hit Washington, which they almost did. Early and his men got to Silver Springs, Maryland, within about a dozen miles of the capital. They were driven off by troops from the Army of the Potomac, hastily dispatched by Grant. The battle was watched by an understandably worried President and Mrs. Lincoln.

While Early was trying to take Washington, D.C., the main body of the Army of the Potomac was still trying to take Petersburg, Virginia. Major General Ambrose Burnside, wearer of the sideburns and veteran of First Bull Run, Antietam, Fredericksburg, the Wilderness, Spotsylvania, and Cold Harbor, had a rather novel idea. Dig a 500-foot tunnel beneath the Confederate lines, pack it with explosives, blow a huge hole in the Rebel defenses, and rush in to take the city.

Burnside's men, used to his periodic bursts of energy and offbeat notions, generally laughed at the idea. Grant didn't think much of it but didn't object since it would "keep the men occupied." Major James C. Duane, Meade's chief engineer, said the whole thing was nonsense.

But Pennsylvania coal miners were brought to the site and the digging began. There was little lumber for this impossible task, few tools, and no wheelbarrows. The whole project took about a month, and by that time, the Confederates were getting suspicious that "something was going on beneath their feet." Lee was alerted. Although he was assured that the idea of digging so long a tunnel was preposterous, he told his engineers to consider laying mines if they heard the sound of picks beneath the ground. Apparently, they did not.

On July 30, the four tons of gunpowder now packed into the tunnel were lit by a 98-foot fuse. The earth trembled and an

BLACK TROOPS GO FIRST

At the fight in the Petersburg crater, General Burnside, according to Major William H. Powell, Federal Army, "... wanted to put his colored division in front, and I believe if he had done so it would have been a success. Still I agreed with General Meade as to his objections to that plan. General Meade said if we put the colored troops in front (we had only one division) and it should prove a failure, it would then be said, and very properly, that we were shoving these people ahead to get killed because we did not care anything about them. But that could not be said if we put white troops in front."

Black troops at the siege of Petersburg. Stationed in the most advanced and dangerous position, their job was to alert the Union soldiers behind them of any enemy activity.

enormous mushroom of smoke, fire, debris, and some body parts sprang into the air. More than 250 Confederate soldiers died in the blast. When the smoke cleared, there was an awesome crater—250 feet long, 70 feet wide, and 30 feet deep.

That was the first part of Burnside's plan. Now things began to fall apart. It took about an hour for Federal troops to move and when they did, they rushed down into the great hole, for some reason, rather than around it. Naturally, when they got to the other end of the crater, there was no way to rush up. No one, of course, had ladders. The men in the crater were now target practice for the enemy, and by early afternoon, Federal soldiers raised the white flag.

About 1,000 died, including scores of black troops shot while trying to surrender, and more than 1,000 bluecoats were taken prisoner. Burnside's bizarre scheme was done. Grant said it was the "saddest affair" he had ever encountered in the war. He granted Burnside "extended leave," and he was never recalled to active duty.

Thousands of black soldiers fought for the Union during the Civil War, not only at Petersburg but in other major battles and small skirmishes as well. Many of them were free Northerners. The Massachusetts 54th, for example, was made up a majority of free black men. Others were former slaves liberated by the U.S. Army in Louisiana and South Carolina, or those who had been freed by their masters in such states as Kentucky, Maryland, Missouri, Tennessee, and in western Virginia. The South, however, refused to accept blacks—any blacks, not just runaway slaves—as soldiers. Acceptance would have put them on an equal footing with their white counterparts. In fact, the Confederates were often not against killing black soldiers who tried to surrender or those taken as prisoners of war. One of the worst examples of this practice was the massacre at Fort Pillow, Tennessee, in the spring of 1864. Confederates led by Nathan Bedford Forrest, later the founder of the hate-driven, antiblack Klu Klux Klan, attacked this minor Federal outpost. About 90 percent of the black Union soldiers were killed, some burned to death, some buried alive, even though they surrendered. Only about 25 percent of the fort's white soldiers died.

If many black soldiers were killed instead of taken prisoner, what happened to white soldiers who were captured? What of those taken during the tunnel massacre and in other battles during the Civil War? What happened to them?

A large part of the Civil War's casualty lists included those sent to prison camps in both the North and South. During the Civil

THE MASSACRE AT FORT PILLOW

OFFICIAL CONFIRMATION OF THE REPORT.

THREE HUNDRED BLACK SOLDIERS MURDERED AFTER SURRENDER

FIFTY-THREE WHITE SOLDIERS KILLED AND ONE HUNDRED WOUNDED

RETALIATION TO BE MADE

Headlines in a Northern newspaper announce the confirmation of reports about the shameful murder of captured Union troops, most of whom were black.

War, about 194,000 Federal troops and about 215,000 Confederates fell into this category. About 30,000 Yanks and some 26,000 Rebels died there. In the early years of the war, there were few camps because there were few prisoners actually imprisoned. Both sides generally allowed the captured men to return to their homes, on their word not to return to the war, or quickly arranged for prisoner exchanges after a battle. This exchange system fell apart in 1863, however, due mainly to the North's decision to use runaway slaves in the military. The South refused to honor them with the status of soldier. Lee would not allow prisoner exchanges if they involved blacks. He said, "Negroes belonging to our citizens are not considered subjects of exchange." Grant, however, insisted that blacks be treated as were whites.

After 1863, captured men were generally sent to prison camps, which were usually poorly constructed and poorly maintained. Prisoners were subjected to all sorts of abuses, some intended, some the result of the general scarcity of everything in the country.

It is probably safe to say that conditions in all the prison camps, both North and South, throughout the Civil War were shocking. At Elmira, New York, for instance, an average of 10 prisoners died each day, mostly from cold, no heat, inadequate clothing, and a horribly polluted sewage system. The camp was open for just six months. During that time, 12,000 Rebel prisoners passed through and nearly 3,000 died there.

But even the horrors of Elmira cannot compare with the one name that came to define all prison camps of that time. It was built in an isolated area in south central Georgia and became known by the name of a nearby settlement—Andersonville.

This 27-acre camp was enclosed by a stockade fence. About 15

feet inside was the "deadline," a single rail atop short wooden posts. That was the entire barrier for the prison camp. Prisoners quickly learned, however, that if they stepped over the deadline, they would be shot. Many were.

The camp was run by a Swiss native with a violent temper, Captain Henry Wirz, later called the most hated man in America. A wound he suffered at Seven Pines in 1862 left him with a useless arm. A rigid disciplinarian, he was later accused of every manner of atrocity. Even without those charges, he would have been hated, just for the conditions at the camp. With food in short supply throughout the South, the prisoners were reduced to the point of starvation. There was very little shelter and almost no medical care. Conditions were so crowded that the water supply became polluted almost instantly. All in all, about 49,000 prisoners entered Andersonville. In less than one year, some 13,000 men died. During one dreadful 24-hour-period, 127 prisoners died of starvation or disease. That totaled one death every 11 minutes.

The notorious prison camp at Andersonville was crowded with more than three times the number of prisoners it was meant to hold. Prisoners' shelters often consisted of shallow holes covered with blankets.

I WAS MERELY OBEYING ORDERS

Captain Henry Wirz, in charge of the military prison at Andersonville, was not the first nor the last military figure to cite obeying orders as a defense. Taken into custody, Wirz requested permission to return to his native Switzerland. "The duties I had to perform were arduous and unpleasant," he declared, "and I am satisfied that no one can or will justly blame me for things that happened here and which were beyond my power to control." The American people disagreed.

After Sherman captured Atlanta in 1864, Andersonville was evacuated. Wirz was arrested and taken to Washington for trial. The outcome, of course, was never in doubt. Unrepentant, Wirz stood on the gallows on November 10, 1865, and listened as the presiding officer read the order of execution. Then he said calmly, "I know what orders are, Major. And I am being hanged for obeying them." As the rope slid around his neck, soldiers lining the walls of the Old Capitol Prison chanted, "Andersonville, Andersonville."

The warm, languid days of the Virginia summer wore on. Exhausted from long months of fighting, weary of the long war, the opposing armies rested and warily watched the movements of the other. Some of the movements were not totally related to the war. In both Richmond and Petersburg, Confederate soldiers sometimes slipped away from the trenches for a few hours in town, especially if a dance was being held. Young ladies dressed in what finery was still to be found strolled the wide streets of a summer evening. Confederate escorts in tow, they sometimes waved across the parapet at the watching Yankee soldiers. On such evenings, by unspoken agreement, pickets on either side did not fire their rifles until the young ladies went home.

Stalled at Petersburg, Grant was bothered by the persistent presence of Jubal Early, "Old Jube," as his men called him. Although he had been driven away from Washington, Early was still in the upper end of Virginia's Shenandoah Valley. Unable to see to it himself, Grant put Major General Philip H. Sheridan in charge of getting rid of Early and taking the Shenandoah Valley out of the war. Grant meant that literally. He wanted the rich farmlands of the South destroyed so that they could no longer support the Confederate Army.

In late September, Sheridan met and badly defeated the outnumbered Early at Winchester, Virginia. Then the Yankee troops, under orders, set about destroying the countryside. This brought all notions of romanticized war—if, indeed, any still existed—to a halt. In retaliation, small guerrilla bands of Southern troops began harrassing the Federals, raiding their outposts, burning wagon trains, shooting the sentries. Prisoners taken were usually hanged on the spot.

In the middle of October, Early surprised Sheridan's army, once again near Winchester, sending the Federals down the road in a disorganized retreat. Furious, Sheridan regrouped his forces and counterattacked. The overwhelming victory made it clear that Early and the South would no longer be a threat in the Shenandoah.

It was also clear that no one was winning the battle for Petersburg or Richmond. At least, not this year. Both these courageous armies had worn each other out.

The two sides settled in for the winter. Overall, the Federal army was relatively well fed and clothed. Lee's men were near to starving, with the ruined countryside offering little relief. There was food, though, in North Carolina and Georgia, but the

DAMN THE TORPEDOES!

While Grant and Lee were glaring at each other in Petersburg, 63-year-old Admiral David Farragut, hero of New Orleans, was trying to enter Mobile Bay, Alabama, which was still open to Confederate shipping. On August 5, with 18 ships, he sailed into the bay. When his lead ship was struck by mines, called torpedoes, the rest of the fleet stopped in alarm. Then, Farragut, who suffered from such dizziness that he had to be strapped to the mast in order to stand up, shouted his famous words: "Damn the torpedoes! Full speed ahead!"

Farragut swung his own ship, the *Hartford*, across the mines, which failed to explode. The rest of his fleet followed. He took Mobile Bay, along with the largest Confederate ironclad afloat, the *Tennessee*.

That was the highlight of Farragut's career, for poor health forced him from service. He was made a full admiral in 1866 and died in 1870.

This somewhat imaginative picture shows the aging Farragut as a younger man standing easily in the rigging while his ship leads a Union fleet through mine-strewn Mobile Bay.

governors of those states would not cooperate with the Rebel government by shipping it elsewhere.

There was no time or cause for the South to celebrate as the year drew to a close. And yet Lee could remind his gallant Army of Virginia, now about 57,000 in number, of one thing. Despite all that Grant and the Army of the Potomac, now numbering about 120,000, could throw at them, they had survived. The South would fight again, another day.

Sherman, Atlanta, and War's End:

May 1864 - April 1865

In 1864, the third year of the American Civil War, the house was still woefully divided, the outcome still uncertain.

How were they faring, these two parts of the divided house? When the war began, about 20 million people lived in the North, about one-fifth foreign born. Most of them lived on farms and in small towns, but the population was steadily shifting to the cities. In waging a long and costly war, the North was able to tap vast resources that the South could never equal. The North had six times as many manufacturing plants and 12 times as many factory workers as did the Southern states. The rich farmlands of the Midwest gave the region an edge in farm production, especially of food crops, as well.

But it is important to remember that all through the war, the North never spoke as one voice. Its people, of many diverse backgrounds, never all agreed on exactly why they were fighting a war, or even if it was worth it. And, especially in the early years, as defeat piled upon defeat, many began to question the wisdom of continuing the fighting at all. It is at least partly the political genius of Abraham Lincoln that the North, nearing war's end, could find one voice and one will to fight for the ideal of Union above all.

The South was far more unified in its will and purpose. Southerners, simply put, were fighting for a way of life, their very

6

existence, which would—as it did—die without victory. In a sense, the Southern way of life was partly the cause of its own defeat. Slavery was geared to a plantation economy, not a war economy. Slavery kept the South from developing a citizen class of skilled workers. Without a manufacturing base, the Confederacy was doomed to defeat. No amount of valor or patriotism could overcome that simple fact.

The North had another, more subtle edge over the South as it related to winning a war. Both presidents—Abraham Lincoln and Jefferson Davis—were strong men of determination and totally devoted to the cause for which they fought. But where Davis possessed an iron will that rarely bent, Lincoln was more flexible. His political instincts and abilities had taught him how to win without making enemies of his opposition. He could make use of the talents of those around him even when they considered themselves—as they often did—his betters. Davis had never learned this rough-and-tumble art of politics. He lacked humor and tact and although he had a logical mind and many fine abilities, he found it difficult to be patient. As a result, Lincoln's Cabinet served him well through the war, whereas Davis's did not, and Davis often seemed to be working alone.

As the war rolled into its third year and Grant and Lee battled each other in Virginia, William Tecumseh Sherman began his march through Georgia on May 7, 1864. He was entrusted with a vital part of Grant's master plan. While the Army of the Potomac battled Lee, Sherman would seize Atlanta, which was an important transportation hub and a growing manufacturing center. In so doing, he would destroy the combined Confederate armies of Tennessee and Mississippi under command of Joseph E. Johnston. With Atlanta secured, Sherman would march north through the Carolinas and eventually meet up with a victorious—it was hoped—Grant and the Army of the Potomac.

Thus began an 11-month masterful series of cat-and-mouse maneuvers by rival commanders, Sherman and Johnston. The Georgia and Carolina campaigns eventually brought Sherman victory. They brought him two other things as well—cheers from Southern blacks, who saw him as a great liberator, and the everlasting hatred of most Southern whites.

William Tecumseh Sherman (1820–91) was an especially odd character in a military full of odd characters. He generally looked on the scruffy side, a rather tall scarecrow of a man with nervous hands, sandy hair that seemed never to have felt a comb, and a stiff red beard. As he began his march toward Atlanta, he was 44 years old and a major general.

Sherman's March to the Sea, which began on November 15, 1864, covered over 400 miles of Confederate territory and ended with the capture of Savannah on December 21.

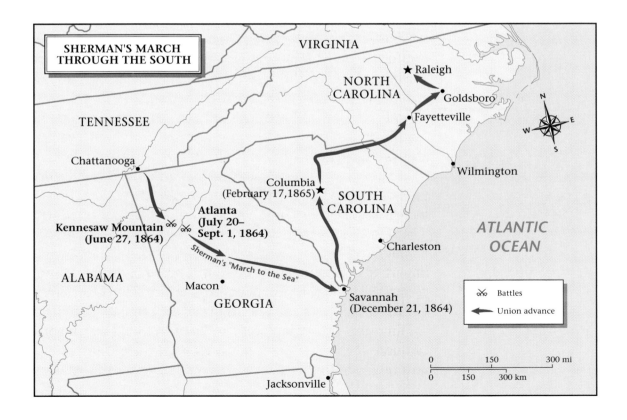

SHERMAN'S MARCH THROUGH THE SOUTH

VIRGINIA

★ Raleigh

NORTH CAROLINA

● Goldsboro

● Fayetteville

TENNESSEE

● Wilmington

Chattanooga ●

Columbia (February 17,1865) ★

SOUTH CAROLINA

Atlanta (July 20– Sept. 1, 1864)

Kennesaw Mountain ✂ ✂ (June 27, 1864)

ATLANTIC OCEAN

● Charleston

Sherman's "March to the Sea"

ALABAMA

Macon ●

GEORGIA

Savannah (December 21, 1864)

✂ Battles

← Union advance

Jacksonville ●

0   150   300 mi
0   150   300 km

Born in Lancaster, Ohio, he graduated from West Point in 1840, sixth in his class. In 1850, he married Ellen Ewing. She was the daughter of U.S. Senator Thomas Ewing of Ohio, who was also Sherman's guardian. Sherman's own father had died when he was very young. Sherman and his wife had eight children. His favorite was Willy, who died of typhoid fever at the age of nine. Sherman was devastated and told his wife, "With Willy dies in me all real ambition."

Sherman was a courageous, determined leader, as well as a nervous and irritable man. He talked constantly and ate little. At night before a battle, he often sat around the campfire in red flannel long johns and an old bathrobe. A lawyer, he was devoted to the cause of law and order and to the Union, although not necessarily to the cause of democracy, which he regarded as rule by the mob. And although he accepted slavery as a legalized institution in the South, he was totally against secession. He

TRUSTED FRIENDS

Sherman was Grant's most trusted lieutenant and a good friend. Early in the war, Sherman had come close to a breakdown after blaming himself for losing too many men in battle. Grant had been his strength during that dark period. Sherman explained their loyalty in this way: "Grant stood by me when I was crazy, and I stood by him when he was drunk; and now we stand by each other always."

General Sherman takes a few moments from his military duties to pose for a photograph.

regarded all those who withdrew from the Union as criminals who should be treated as such.

Although much of the South viewed Sherman's tactics as ruthless and himself as nothing less than the devil, Sherman was, in fact, ruthless because he felt he had to be. He understood that the North would be victorious only if it destroyed the ability of the South to make war. He may have used emotional and economic tactics against enemy civilians, but he did not, as some did on both sides, shoot them or kill prisoners of war. Some historians regard him as brilliant for just that reason: He was able to break the back of the rebellion without killing civilians or bombing them, a tactic often used in warfare today.

Grant placed his utmost trust in his longtime friend. As Sherman moved south from Chattanooga into northern Georgia that early May of 1864, his Grand Army of the West marched nearly 100,000 strong. It was divided into three columns: in the center, the Army of the Cumberland, headed by George "Pap" Thomas, the Rock of Chickamauga; on the right, the Army of the Tennessee under James McPherson; on the left, John Schofield's Army of the Ohio.

Realistically, Johnston and his Confederates had little hope of defeating Sherman. They were outsupplied, outgunned, and outgeneraled, to say nothing of being outnumbered nearly two to one. But they could hope to slow down Sherman's progress to Atlanta. Which is exactly what they did.

Through the terrible heat of the southern summer, eaten alive by insects and made miserable by the unrelenting dirt and dust, Sherman and Johnston sparred with each other in the wooded hillsides of northern Georgia. The Yankees were not at as much of a disadvantage as might be assumed, however, for Sherman knew this area quite well. He had surveyed much of it as a young lieutenant. "I knew Georgia better than the rebels did," he boasted.

By not attacking Johnston's forces head on, but hitting them on the flanks in small skirmishes, Sherman made slow but steady progress southward. He grew frustrated, however, with the pace. When in mid-June he faced Johnston across Kennesaw Mountain, about 20 miles from Atlanta, Sherman decided on an all-out attack. "We are supposed to be on the offensive," he growled.

On June 27, with Grant still stalled at Petersburg, Sherman and 13,000 troops hit Johnston's army head on. It was a mistake. Although Sherman would never admit it, he never repeated it either. Johnston's men were too well entrenched for such an assault. In this, the biggest battle of Sherman's campaign so far, he lost more than 2,000, killed, wounded, or missing. On this day also, President Lincoln formally accepted nomination for a second term.

Sherman went back to his hit-'em-at-the-flank maneuvers. By late July, he had backed Johnston and his army to within sight of the city of Atlanta. Now, President Jefferson Davis fired General Johnston. His dismissal notice said, "... as you failed to arrest the advance of the enemy to the vicinity of Atlanta ... and express no

NOTHING STOOD IN HIS WAY

Sherman was determined to get to Atlanta, no matter what. A few days before the battle at Kennesaw Mountain, his troops were making progress but not as fast as he would have liked. HIs comment at the time was:"A fresh furrow in a plowed field will stop the whole column! We are on the offensive and must assail and not defend."

confidence that you can defeat or repel him, you are hereby relieved from the command of the Army and Department of Tennessee..."

Davis had long disliked Johnston anyway, blaming him for the failure at Vicksburg. Johnston, of course, felt differently. He had not stopped Sherman, but he certainly had stalled him. Sherman had not taken Atlanta nor had he destroyed Johnston's army. Johnston believed that outnumbered as he was, the only possible game to play was to wait and let Sherman's army, so far from home, come to the end of its supply line.

But Davis had a war to win now. To that end he put General John Bell Hood in Johnston's place. Hood was certainly a fighter —Second Bull Run, Antietam, Fredericksburg, Gettysburg, where he lost the use of one arm, and Chickamauga, where he lost a leg. He rode his horse strapped to the saddle.

So, the cautious, careful Johnston was replaced with the impetuous, daring Hood. Sherman was delighted. He was sure now that Hood would attack him head on. In those circumstances, Sherman was certain he would win. True to his reputation, Hood hit the Federals on July 20, less than two days after taking command. He hit them hard at Peachtree Creek, north of Atlanta, and was driven back.

The battle for Atlanta itself began on July 22, 1864. Once again, Hood was driven back, with losses of several thousand. Hood tried a third time. On July 28, he hit Sherman at Ezra Church, west of the city. Once more he failed. Falling back to Atlanta, Hood counted his losses—about 20,000 men, or a third of his army, killed, wounded, or missing in a week.

It might be thought that the impatient Sherman would now have pressed forward, smashed Hood, and occupied the city. The Confederate troops thought he would as they waited nervously in the trenches. But Sherman made no such move. Instead, he waited, content to cut off rail lines and food supplies, starving

The exceptionally strong fortifications surrounding Atlanta helped the Confederates to hold off Union troops for over a month.

the isolated city and generally getting on everyone's nerves.

The siege went on for more than a month. On August 31, it ended. Sherman sent most of his army at Hood's lines south of the city. On September 1, the Confederate troops hastily withdrew. On September 2, Sherman and the Federals occupied Atlanta. "That agony is over," wrote diarist Mary Chesnut. "There is no hope but we will try to have no fear." Wrote Sherman, "Atlanta is ours and fairly won."

Sherman had accomplished half of Grant's master plan for him. He had taken the city of Atlanta. Now he set out to make an example of it. "I have deemed it to the interest of the United States that the citizens now residing in Atlanta should remove, those who prefer it to go South and the rest North." With this edict, about 1,600 white citizens were forced to leave their homes and possessions, taking with them an everlasting hatred of William Tecumseh Sherman. The general was unmoved. "If the people raise a howl against my barbarity and cruelty," he said, "I will answer that war is war and not popularity-seeking."

Sherman's taking of Atlanta had profound consequences not only for the final outcome of the war, but for the reelection of Abraham Lincoln. In late 1864, the President's prospects for a second term looked dim. Actually, they had never looked great in the first place. In private, Lincoln himself expressed doubts that he would win. "I am going to be beaten," he said, "and unless some great change takes place, badly beaten." He had a lot going against him. The country was in the midst of a civil war that wasn't being won, it seemed, by his side. For all his promises, Grant wasn't winning battles and his casualty figures were staggering. In addition, the Democrats, whose candidate was General George B. McClellan, were calling for peace before Union, in effect offering the South its independence.

Many Northerners were deeply disturbed and discontented because of the length of the war and the elusiveness of victory. Lincoln needed some sign for his war-weary people who were having doubts that victory could ever come. Sherman and his siege of Atlanta gave him that sign.

On November 8, 1864, a nervous President awaited the election returns. He was very concerned about the soldiers' vote. Would they back McClellan, their old—and beloved—general, whom Lincoln himself had dismissed from command? The answer was no. The Federal military solidly voted for Lincoln, putting aside their admiration for McClellan for their loyalty to the Union.

Lincoln won 55 percent of the popular vote, carried all but three states—Delaware, Kentucky, and New Jersey, and took 212 electoral votes to McClellan's 21. The Confederate states, of course, did not take part in the election. In effect, the people of the North had told Lincoln to carry on the war and to carry it on to victory. Now, it would be just a question of time.

After evacuating Atlanta, Hood and his army tried to lure Sherman out of the city by marching northward into Tennessee. The Confederates would later be defeated at Nashville.

Sherman did not follow Hood because he had another plan in mind. It was daring and some thought foolhardy. While Hood was heading north, he would head southeast, toward Savannah and the sea. Cut off from his own base of supply and from communication with Washington, his army would live off the land. By moving some 60,000 soldiers across Georgia at will, Sherman would show up the helplessness of the Confederacy and hasten the war's end. He believed that victory was attained not just on the battlefield but when the will of the enemy's citizens to back the war was crushed.

And so, on November 15, 1864, Sherman and his army set out on their never-to-be-forgotten March to the Sea. First, he ordered the burning of about one-third of Atlanta, but only those buildings that might be of some aid to any enemy military. Hood's retreating troops had already destroyed as much as they could of whatever might be of use to the Federals. However, since so much of the city was already empty and the Union soldiers were not necessarily careful about what they set on fire, a good deal of Atlanta went up in smoke.

A little more than a month later, on December 21, Sherman

Destroying means of communication and movement of supplies was an important part of Sherman's plan to lower the South's morale and end the war. Here his men destroy railroad tracks after leaving Atlanta.

occupied the city of Savannah. His 60,000-man army had cut a wide path through the state of Georgia, taking what they wanted, laying waste to what they did not want. Some said it was like one gigantic terrible picnic rather than an army on the march. When it ended, the Grand Army of the West had crossed some 425 miles of enemy territory and caused some $100 million dollars worth of damage. Wrote Mary Chesnut in her diary, "They say no living thing is found in Sherman's track."

It was an ugly march. Sherman may not have wanted his soldiers to act in this unruly, destructive manner, but to his mind, this was war, and war meant destroying the enemy. He was determined to bring the South to its knees, and so he did.

The last year of the war opened on a North now confident of victory and a South with yet a small glimmer of hope. On January 31, 1865, the U.S. Congress submitted the Thirteenth Constitutional Amendment to the states for ratification. It said, "Neither slavery nor involuntary servitude, except as a

This pleasant residence, the home of a wealthy citizen, was taken over by General Sherman for his Savannah headquarters.

punishment for a crime whereof the party shall have been duly convicted, shall exist within the United States, or any place subject to their jurisdiction." With its ratification on December 6 of that year, slavery was no longer legal in the United States.

On February 10, four days after Lee was named general in chief of the Confederate armies, Sherman began to move north to the Carolinas. He was only lightly opposed. On February 17, he entered the South Carolina capital of Columbia. That night it was destroyed by fire. Sherman said the fleeing Rebels set the fires; Confederates blamed the Yanks. The following day, the

HEALING WORDS

Said Lincoln at his second inauguration, March 4, 1865: "Fondly do we hope—fervently do we pray—that this mighty scourge of war may speedily pass away ....With malice towards none; with charity for all; with firmness in the right as God gives us to see the right, let us strive on to finish the work we are in; to bind up the nation's wounds; to care for him who shall have borne the battle and for his widow, and his orphan—to do all which may achieve and cherish a just and lasting peace among ourselves, and with all nations."

On the way home to the White House after the ceremony, Lincoln remarked, "I am a tired man. Sometimes I think I am the tiredest man on earth."

In spite of cold and windy weather, a large crowd attended Lincoln's second inauguration.

Federals captured Charleston, and once again Fort Sumter was back in the Union.

It was a cold and windy day in Washington, D.C., when Lincoln was inaugurated for a second term on March 4, 1865. In the background stood the now completed U.S. Capitol with its new iron dome. The end of the war seemed close at hand, and the President was gentle.

But the war was not yet over. On March 27–28, Lincoln met with Generals Grant and Sherman aboard the *River Queen* at City Point, Virginia. The President did not discuss final plans for the defeat of the Confederacy. Instead, he wanted ideas on how to rebuild the battered nation. Sherman was much impressed. The South, however, was not. Far from giving up, Southern leaders, such as the governor of Virginia, called for every man to arm himself as the Federals approached.

For some nine months, Grant and Lee had been waiting it out at Petersburg. Lee's army was shrinking. Thousands had deserted. When Lee called for more troops and supplies, Davis could only answer that there were none to send. Finally, Lee asked that slaves be armed to defend the Confederacy. This was so authorized on March 13, only because, said the Richmond *Examiner*, "the country will not deny General Lee anything he may ask for."

But there was just not enough of anything. Grant now had an

THE UNMARKED GRAVE

Lee's trusted aide and courageous general, A.P. (for Ambrose Powell) Hill, was killed at Petersburg on April 2. His remains, along with his cape and sword, were taken to Richmond for burial at his wife's request. But by that time, the city was in flames. Hill's relatives found a cheap coffin and transported his body into Chesterfield County where it was buried in an unmarked grave. Years later the coffin was dug up and returned to Richmond. In 1891 a monument was erected in the city in his memory.

army of some 125,000 men; Lee's troops had shrunk to about 35,000. On April 2, at long last, Grant broke through the stubborn Rebel defense at Petersburg. Lee abandoned the city and moved westward. When the news reached Davis, he and the Confederate government hurriedly vacated Richmond and Federal troops took it over on April 3. Much of the capital had been set afire by the fleeing Confederate army.

If Robert E. Lee realized that the end was near, as indeed he must have, he did not show it. Leaving Petersburg, he led his tired and hungry army toward Amelia Court House. There, he intended to provision his troops and head south to link up with the army of Joseph E. Johnston, whom Lee had reinstated, in North Carolina.

Aware of Lee's intention, Grant did not attack but moved in a parallel line south of the Confederates. Lee reached Amelia Court House to find no supplies, nor hope of any. When he turned south, his way was blocked by Union troops. He turned west, but Grant's pursuit was relentless and overwhelming. And, finally, General Lee and the Army of Northern Virginia found themselves cornered at a little town called Appomattox Court House. They had no food or supplies. They were almost entirely surrounded by the enemy and outnumbered almost four to one.

The inevitable end came on April 9, 1865. Shortly before noon, Lee sent a white flag—it was actually a white towel—and a note to the Union lines. He said to his officers, "There is nothing left for me to do, but to go and see General Grant and I would rather die a thousand deaths."

When Grant received the note, in his customary manner, he said nothing. Half an hour later, Lee waited in the front parlor of Wilmer McLean's house. McLean was a patriotic Southerner and none too happy to lend his home to the proceedings. But it was the best-looking residence in the area, so McLean agreed.

I WAS THERE, WERE YOU?

Years after the surrender at Appomattox Court House was signed, an impossible number of officers claimed they had been present in the 16-by-20-foot parlor of Wilmer McLean. Since no photographer was there and no one had made any sketches, it was impossible to be certain who was there and who wasn't. Many artists later sketched the scene. Probably the three most famous were Thomas Nast, Louis Guillaume, and Thomas Lovell. Nast, the political cartoonist, completed his work 30 years after the surrender. His own son posed for the figure of Grant. French-born Guillaume, a resident of Richmond, made a large error in his painting by putting Grant and Lee at the same table. Actually, they sat about five feet apart. Lovell's work (shown below) is said to be the most accurate as far as room proportions and placement of the figures are concerned. However, he put George Custer—of later Little Bighorn fame—in the parlor, although it is said he was outside in the yard during the surrender.

Lee (seated left) signs the surrender papers while Grant (seated right) does the same.

Grant arrived and the two generals shook hands. Robert E. Lee was attired in a crisp uniform, his sword at his side. Ulysses S. Grant had not been able to find a clean uniform, so he wore the shirt of a private and his boots were mud-splattered. He had no sword. He said later that he meant no disrespect to Lee because of his attire.

The conversation was extraordinarily pleasant. In fact, Grant later admitted he almost forgot the object of the meeting until Lee reminded him.

After Lee's surrender, Confederate soldiers sadly roll up the flag they had followed throughout the war.

To the everlasting credit of both men, the surrender was simple, dignified, and honorable. Confederate officers could keep their personal possessions, horses, and side arms. All troops would be allowed to return to their homes. Grant offered the hungry Confederates food, which Lee gratefully accepted. The victorious general declared that there would be no celebrations to mark the enemy's surrender, although this was largely ignored by his troops.

While Grant had been happy at receiving Lee's note of surrender, now he was sad and depressed. He could not rejoice at the defeat of such a gallant adversary. Indeed, Lee and his Army of Northern Virginia had been unbeatable for four years. They had stood up to all the North could throw at them.

The terms of surrender were signed at about 3 p.m. and both men shook hands once again. Lee left the parlor first, walking into the yard where Federal soldiers came to attention and saluted. Lee saluted in return, sighed, and mounted his beloved horse, Traveller. Now Grant appeared. He walked into the yard, stopped, and removed his hat. His officers did the same. Lee lifted his hat in recognition of the gesture and rode off.

There would be other segments of the Confederate army to surrender over the next several weeks. But the meeting at Appomattox Court House marked the end of the most terrible war fought on American soil. Hundreds of thousands on both sides had died, destruction covered much of the South.

The North had won. The United States of America was reunited. Slavery was finally ended. However, heartache, hatred, bitterness, devastation, and suffering remained. The war was over, but the house was still divided.

Chronology of Important Events:

1863

January 1	Lincoln's Emancipation Proclamation of September 22, 1862, becomes effective.
January 2	End of Battle of Murfreesboro (Stone's River), TN -December 30, 1862-January 2, 1863.
January 26	Joseph Hooker succeeds Ambrose Burnside as commander, Army of the Potomac.
February 2	U.S. Congress authorizes national banking system.
March 25	Burnside appointed commander, Department of the Ohio.
April 30	Grant crosses Mississippi River south of Vicksburg.
May 2	Hooker defeated at Chancellorsville, VA; Stonewall Jackson accidentally shot by own men.
May 10	Jackson dies.
May 13	Joseph E. Johnston assumes command, Confederate troops in Mississippi.
May 17	Grant wins Battle of the Big Black River, MS.
May 19	Grant's attack on Vicksburg repulsed.
May 22	Grant opens siege of Vicksburg.
June 20	West Virginia becomes 35th state.
June 28	George Gordon Meade replaces Hooker as commander, Army of the Potomac.
July 1	Battle of Gettysburg, PA, starts.
July 3	Pickett's Charge repulsed; Battle of Gettysburg ends in Union victory.
July 4	Vicksburg surrenders.
July 5	Lee retreats from Gettysburg.
July 13	New York City draft riots begin.
July 16	Federal troops restore order in New York City.
August 21	William C. Quantrill's Confederate raiders burn Lawrence, KS.

September 2   Burnside occupies Knoxville, TN.

September 9   Federal troops enter Chattanooga, TN.

September 19   Battle of Chickamauga, TN, begins.

September 20   Confederates win Battle of Chickamauga.

September 23   Grant arrives at Chattanooga.

September 27   "Cracker line" supply routes to Chattanooga opened.

October 17   Grant named supreme commander of Federal forces in the West.

November 19   Lincoln delivers Gettysburg Address.

November 23   Battle of Chattanooga begins.

November 25   Federals win Battle of Chattanooga.

December 27   Johnston assumes command, Confederate Army of Tennessee.

1864

February 17   Confederate submarine *H.L.Hunley* sinks U.S.S. *Housatonic*.

February 20   Confederates win Battle of Olustee, FL.

February 22   Confederate cavalry victorious at Okolona, MS.

March 4   Sherman returns to Vicksburg after raid on Meridian, MS.

March 9   Grant promoted to lieutenant general; becomes general in chief, Armies of the United States.

March 18   Sherman takes command of Union armies in the West.

April 10   Archduke Maximilian, puppet of Napoleon III, crowned emperor of Mexico in violation of Monroe Doctrine.

May 4   Grant crosses Rapidan River, VA, to attack Lee.

May 5   Battle of the Wilderness begins.

May 6   James Longstreet halts Grant's offensive in Wilderness. Sherman opens Atlanta campaign against Johnston's Army of Tennessee.

May 7	Grant races Lee to Spotsylvania Court House, VA.
May 10	Lee halts Grant at Spotsylvania.
May 12	Day-long fight at "Bloody Angle" in the Spotsylvania campaign
May 24	Grant and Lee fight at North Anna River, VA.
May 25	Sherman and Johnston fight at New Hope Church, GA.
May 28	Grant and Lee begin 4-day fight at Totopotomoy Creek, VA.
June 3	Lee defeats Grant at Cold Harbor, VA.
June 14	Lt. Gen. Leonidas Polk killed at Pine Mountain, GA.
June 18	Grant opens siege of Petersburg, VA, after assault fails.
June 19	U.S.S. *Kearsarge* sinks Confederate raider *Alabama* off Cherbourg, France.
June 23	Jubal Early opens Confederate campaign in Shenandoah Valley.
June 27	Sherman driven back at Kennesaw Mountain, GA.
July 11	Army of the Potomac reinforcements arrive to protect Washington, D.C., from Early's raid.
July 12	Early withdraws to Shenandoah Valley.
July 17	John Bell Hood replaces Johnston as commander, Army of Tennessee.
July 20	Hood defeated at Peachtree Creek, GA.
July 28	Federals driven back at Deep Bottom, VA. Hood defeated at Ezra Church, GA.
July 30	Federals driven back at Battle of the Crater at siege of Petersburg. Union troops unsuccessful in attempt to free prisoners at Andersonville.
August 5	Farragut victorious in Battle of Mobile Bay, AL.
August 7	Sheridan assumes command of Union forces in Shenandoah.
September 1	Hood evacuates Atlanta. Sherman enters Atlanta the next day.
September 4	Citizens ordered out of Atlanta.
September 19	Sheridan defeats Early at Winchester in Shenandoah.

September 24   Sheridan begins destruction of food crops and livestock in Shenandoah Valley.

October 19   Sheridan drives Confederates from Shenandoah.

October 31   Nevada becomes 36th state in the Union.

November 8   Lincoln wins second term in the White House.

November 15   Sherman burns Atlanta and starts march to the sea.

December 16   Hood defeated at Nashville.

December 21   Sherman occupies Savannah.

1865

January 31   Thirteenth Amendment, abolishing slavery, submitted to the states for ratification.

February 1   Sherman begins invasion of the Carolinas.

February 6   Robert E. Lee appointed commander in chief of all Confederate armies.

February 17   Sherman takes Columbia, capital of South Carolina.

February 18   Federals take Charleston and Fort Sumter.

March 4   Lincoln inaugurated for second term.

March 11   Sherman reaches Fayetteville, NC.

March 17   Federals attack Mobile, AL.

March 23   Sherman takes Goldsboro, NC.

March 28   Lincoln discusses battle plans and possibilities of peace aboard *River Queen* at City Point, VA.

April 2   Grant breaks through Lee's lines at Petersburg; General Hill killed; Lee abandons city; Confederate government flees Richmond.

April 3   Federal troops enter Richmond.

April 9   Lee surrenders Army of Northern Virginia to Grant at Appomattox Court House, VA.

Facts About Key Personalities

Cited below are some of the key figures in the Civil War during the period covered by this book. Listed are their main contributions and/or main theaters of operation during 1863–65. (Abbreviations used throughout are as follows: **CSA**: Confederate States of America; **USA**: United States of America.)

Barton, Clara (1821–1912): Born Massachusetts. Schoolteacher; distributed supplies and cared for wounded during Civil War; American Red Cross founder and first president (1882-1904).

Beauregard, P.G.T. (1818–93): Gen. CSA. Born Louisiana; West Point (1838). Petersburg, Carolinas.

Bragg, Braxton (1817–76): Gen. CSA. Born North Carolina; West Point (1837). Chickamauga, Chattanooga; relieved Dec. 1863; military adviser to Davis (1864–65).

Buford, John (1826–63): Maj. Gen. USA. West Point (1848). Gettysburg.

Burnside, Ambrose E. (1824–81): Maj. Gen. USA. Born Indiana; West Point (1847). Wilderness, Spotsylvania, Cold Harbor, Petersburg; relieved Aug. 1864.

Butler, Benjamin F. (1818–93): Maj. Gen. USA. Born New Hampshire. Military governor of New Orleans, (1862); Army of the James commander (1864–65).

Custer, George A. (1839–76): Maj. Gen. USA. Born Ohio; West Point (1861). Petersburg, Shenandoah Valley, Appomattox; died at famous Battle of Little Bighorn (1876).

Davis, Jefferson (1808–89): President CSA. Born Kentucky; West Point (1828). Resigned from army (1835) when state seceded; fled from Richmond, April 3, 1865.

Dix, Dorothea (1802–87): Born Maine. Served through Civil War as superintendent of women nurses for the Union.

Doubleday, Abner (1819–93): Maj. Gen. USA. Born New York; West Point (1842). Chancellorsville, Gettysburg.

Early, Jubal A. (1816–94): Lt. Gen. CSA. Born Virginia; West Point (1837). Chancellorsville, Gettysburg, Wilderness, Spotsylvania, Cold Harbor, Shenandoah Valley.

Everett, Edward (1794–1865): Born Massachusetts. U.S. senator (1853-54). Delivered speech at Gettysburg prior to Lincoln's Gettysburg Address (Nov. 19, 1863).

Ewell, Richard S. (1817–82): Lt. Gen. CSA. Born Georgetown, D.C. West Point (1840). Gettysburg, Wilderness, Spotsylvania, defense of Richmond.

Farragut, David G. (1801–70): Vice Adm. USA. Born Tennessee. Captured New Orleans (1862). Battle of Mobile Bay.

Grant, Ulysses S. (1822–85): Gen. USA. Born Ohio; West Point (1843). Vicksburg, Chattanooga. Named general in chief of Union armies, March 1864; directed Army of the Potomac (1864–65); received Lee's surrender at Appomattox Court House, April 9, 1865.

Halleck, Henry W. (1815–72): Maj. Gen. USA. Born New York; West Point (1839). General in chief of Union armies, (1862–64); chief of staff (1864–65).

Hill, Ambrose P. (1825–65): Lt. Gen. CSA. Born Virginia; West Point (1847). Chancellorsville, Gettysburg, Wilderness, Cold Harbor, killed at Petersburg, April 2.

Hooker, Joseph (Fighting Joe) (1814–79); Maj. Gen. USA. Born Massachusetts; West Point (1837). Chancellorsville, Atlanta, March to the Sea, Carolinas; resigned his command July 28, 1864.

Jackson, Thomas J. "Stonewall" (1824–63): Lt. Gen. CSA. Born in what is now West Virginia; West Point (1846). Chancellorsville, accidentally shot by his own men, May 2, died May 10.

Johnston, Joseph E. (1807–91): Gen. CSA. Born Virginia; West Point (1829). Army of Tennessee commander, Atlanta, Carolinas. Surrendered to Sherman, April 26, 1865.

Lee, Robert E. (1807–70): Gen. CSA. Born Virginia; West Point (1829). Resigned U.S. Army 1861 to command Virginia troops; led Army of Northern Virginia: Peninsula campaign to Appomattox. Named Confederate general in chief, Feb. 6, 1865; surrendered to Grant, Appomattox Court House, April 9, 1865.

Lincoln, Abraham (1809–65): 16th president of the United States (1861–65); born Kentucky. Shot at Ford's Theatre, Washington, DC, April 14, by John Wilkes Booth, died next day.

Longstreet, James (1821–1904): Lt. Gen. CSA. Born South Carolina, West Point (1842). Gettysburg, Chickamauga, Knoxville, Wilderness, Petersburg, Appomattox.

McClellan, George G. (1826–85): Maj. Gen. USA. Born Pennsylvania; West Point (1846). Democratic candidate opposing Lincoln (1864).

Meade, George C. (1815–72): Maj. Gen. USA. Born Spain; West Point (1835). Chancellorsville, Army of the Potomac commander, Gettysburg to Appomattox.

Pemberton, John C. (1814–81): Lt. Gen. CSA. Born Pennsylvania; West Point (1837). Entered Confederate service (1861); Vicksburg defense; surrendered to Grant (1863).

Pickett, George E. (1825–75): Maj. Gen. CSA. Born Virginia; West Point (1846). Led famous, doomed charge at Gettysburg (1863).

Pleasonton, Alfred (1824–97): Maj. Gen. USA. Born Washington, D.C. Chancellorsville, Gettysburg; transferred to Missouri, helped defeat last Confederate efforts in West.

Polk, Leonadis (1806–64): Lt. Gen. Born North Carolina; West Point (1825). Murfreesboro, Chickamauga, Atlanta; killed at Pine Mountain, Georgia.

Porter, David Dixon (1813–91): Rear Adm. USA. Born Pennsylvania. Vicksburg, commanded North Atlantic blockade.

Quantrill, William C. (1837–65): Col. CSA. Born Ohio. Guerrilla commander; led raids in Kansas (1863).

Rosecrans, William S. (1819–98): Maj. Gen. USA. Born Ohio; West Point (1842). Murfreesboro, Chickamauga; relieved Oct. 1863.

Sheridan, Philip H. (1831–88): Maj. Gen. USA. Born New York; West Point (1853). Murfreesboro, Chickamauga, Chattanooga, Wilderness, Spotsylvania, Richmond raid, Cold Harbor; Army of the Tennessee commander, Appomattox.

Sherman, William Tecumseh (1820–91): Maj. Gen. USA. Born Ohio; West Point (1840). Vicksburg; Army of the Tennessee commander, Chattanooga; Mississippi commander, Atlanta, March to the Sea, Carolinas.

Sickles, Daniel E. (1825–1914): Maj. Gen. USA. Born New York. Chancellorsville, Gettysburg (lost right leg).

Sigel, Franz (1824–1902): Maj. Gen. USA. Born Baden, Germany; emigrated to New York (1852). Dept. of West Virginia commander.

Stuart, James Ewell Brown (Jeb) (1833–64): Maj. Gen. CSA. Born Virginia; West Point (1854). Chancellorsville, Gettysburg raid, Wilderness, Spotsylvania.

Thomas, George H. (1816–70): Maj. Gen. USA. Born Virginia; West Point (1840). Chickamauga (earned nickname "Rock of Chickamauga"), Chattanooga, Atlanta.

Warren, Gouverneur K. (1830–82): Maj. Gen. USA. Born New York. Gettysburg, Wilderness, Spotsylvania, Cold Harbor, Petersburg.

Glossary

artillery   Weapons used by a military force; an army unit armed with artillery.

barricade   In war, an obstruction erected to stop the advance of an enemy force.

blockade   Isolation of a particular enemy area, such as a harbor, by a warring nation to prevent supplies and equipment from entering.

bluff   A high, steep bank, a cliff.

bombardment   A vigorous assault, particularly with artillery, on an enemy.

courier   A message bearer, such as a member of the diplomatic service who delivers secret or important messages to another country.

czar   Ruler of Russia until the 1917 revolution.

desertion   The abandoning of one's post or duties, as in the military, without authority.

dictator   A ruler with absolute power.

emancipation   The act of freeing from bondage or restraint, as freeing slaves

gunboat   An armed ship.

homefront   Civilian activity during a war.

ironclad   During the Civil War, a ship covered with protective armor.

proclamation   An official public announcement.

skirmish   A brief minor military fight.

tyrant   An absolute ruler who uses power brutally.

whistle-stop   A small station or community where trains stop only on signal.

Bibliography

Bradford, Ned. *Battles and Leaders of the Civil War.* New York: Appleton, 1956.

Catton, Bruce. *The American Heritage New History of the Civil War.* New York: Viking, 1996.

Commager, Henry Steele. *The Blue and the Gray.* New York: Bobbs-Merrill, 1950.

_____. *Documents of American History*, Vol 1. Upper Saddle River, NJ: Prentice Hall, 1988.

Davis, William C., ed. *The Civil War.* Alexandria, VA: Time-Life Books, 1983, 28 vols.

Gruver, Rebecca Brooks. *An American History,* Vol. 1. London: Addison-Wesley, 1972.

Long, E.B. *The Civil War Day by Day: An Almanac 1861–1865.* New York: Doubleday, 1971.

McPherson, James M. *For Cause & Comrades: Why Men Fought in the Civil War.* New York: Oxford Univ. Press, 1997.

Ward, Geoffrey C. *The Civil War: An Illustrated History.* New York: Knopf, 1990.

Further Reading

Arnold, James R. *Grant Wins the War: Decision at Vicksburg.* New York: Wiley, 1997.

Astor, Gerald. *The Right to Fight: A History of African Americans in the Military.* Novato, CA: Presidio Press, 1998.

Corrick, James A. *The Battle of Gettysburg.* San Diego, CA: Lucent, 1996.

Eicher, David. *Mystic Chords of Memory: Civil War Battlefields and Historic Sites Recaptured.* Baton Rouge, LA: Louisiana State University Press, 1998.

Gallagher, Gary (ed.) *The Wilderness Campaign.* Chapel Hill, NC: University of North Carolina Press, 1997.

Gordon, Lesley J. *General George E. Pickett in Life and Legend.* Chapel Hill, NC: University of North Carolina Press, 1998.

Harmon, Dan. *Civil War Leaders.* Broomall, PA: Chelsea House, 1998.

Haskins, Jim. *Black, Blue, and Gray: African Americans in the Civil War.* Old Tappan, NJ: Simon & Schuster, 1998.

Kelly, Orr, and Kelly, Mary Davies. *Dreams End: Two Iowa Brothers in the Civil War.* New York: Kodansha America, 1998.

Marrin, Albert. *Unconditional Surrender: U.S. Grant and the Civil War.* Old Tappan, NJ: Simon & Schuster, 1994.

Page, Dave. *Ship vs. Shore: Engagements between Land and Sea.* Nashville, TN: Rutledge Hill Press, 1994.

Palmer, Michael A. *Lee Moves North.* New York: Wiley, 1998.

Whitelaw, Nancy. *Clara Barton: Civil War Nurse.* Springfield, NJ: Enslow, 1997.

Websites

Here are a few suggested websites with information relevant to the contents of this book. The authors and the editors take no responsibility for the accuracy of any information found on the Internet. Nor can we guarantee the availability of any website.

Abraham Lincoln Online
Everything about Honest Abe, from speeches to photographs and a Quiz of the Month. You can even join an online discussion.
http://www.netins.net/showcase/creative/lincoln.html

American Civil War Texts
Electronic texts made available by the University of Virginia.
http://etext.lib.virginia.edu/subjects/civilwar.html

Civil War: An Illinois Soldier
The memoirs, diary, and life of Private Jefferson Moses, Company G, 93rd Illinois Volunteers.
http://www.ioweb.com/civilwar/

Civil War Information, Documents and Archive
Large archive of primary sources and links to material on the Web.
http://users.iamdigex.net/bdboyle/cw.html

Civil War Soldiers & Sailors System
A database of 235,000 searchable records for soldiers serving in the United States Colored Troops during the Civil War.
http://www.itd.nps.gov/cwss/

Jews in the Civil War
Photographs, letters, and essays recounting the history of Jews fighting in the Civil War.
http://www.jewish-history.com/jewish.htm

Letters from an Iowa Soldier in the Civil War
Rich details of the war and life in Union camps. Actual letters written home by young Private Newton Scott.
http://bob.ucsc.edu/civil-war-letters/home.html

Valley of the Shadow—Two Communities in the American Civil War
Online exhibition from the University of Virginia.
http://jefferson.village.virginia.edu/vshadow2/

Zoom In on the Civil War
Exploring history through artifacts.
http://www.ilt.columbia.edu/k12/history/gb/civilhome.html

Index

Note: Page numbers in italics indicate illustrations or maps.

Index

Index

Index

Acknowledgments

Cover: The Granger Collection; p.3 "Surrender at Appomattox" by Thomas Lovell, ©1988 The Greenwich Workshop, Inc. Trumbull, CT; p.7 The Granger Collection; p.8 Massachusetts Commandery Military, Order of the Loyal Legion and the US Army Military Hisotry Institute; p.11 Courtesy the Boston Athenaeum; p.14 CORBIS/Bettmann; p.16 ©North Wind Pictures; p.19 Virgina Military Institute Archives; p.26 ©North Wind Pictures; pp.31, 32 The Granger Collection; p.34 CORBIS/Digital Stock; p.37 CORBIS; p.45 "Saving The Flag" Painting by Don Troiani, Photo Courtesy of Historical Art Prints, Ltd.; p.48 SV-Library; p.49 CORBIS/Bettmann; pp.51, 53 Brown Brothers; p.55 CORBIS; p.57 CORBIS/Medford Historical Society Collection; p.62 Culver Pictures, Inc.; p.65 National Archives; p.66 Archive Photos; p.69 CORBIS/Medford Historical Society Collection; pp.71, 74 Library of Congress; p.78 Archive Photos; p.80 ©Stock Montage; pp.84, 88 CORBIS; p.89 CORBIS/Bettmann; p.91 SV-Library; p.92 CORBIS; p.95 "Surrender at Appomattox" by Thomas Lovell, ©1988 The Greenwich Workshop, Inc. Trumbull, CT; p.96 West Point Museum Collection, United States Military Academy.

Map design & production: Tina Graziano, MapQuest.com